Worlds Together

A Journey Into Multicultural Literature

Patricia Richard-Amato

Wendy Abbott Hansen

Addison-Wesley

Reading, Massachusetts • Menlo Park, California • New York
Don Mills, Ontario • Wokingham, England • Amsterdam • Bonn • Sydney
Singapore • Tokyo • Madrid • San Juan • Paris • Seoul, Korea • Milan
• Mexico City • Taipei, Taiwan

For Daniel Hansen,
who has taught us
what it means to be a hero.

A PUBLICATION OF THE WORLD LANGUAGE DIVISION

Executive Editor: Elinor Chamas
Editorial Development: Karen Howse
Cover and Text Design: Brown Publishing Network, Inc.
   Chris Hammill Paul
Art Direction/Production: Brown Publishing Network, Inc.
   Trelawney Goodell, Susan Unger, Diana Maloney
Production/Manufacturing: James W. Gibbons

ISBN: 0-201-82386-1
1 2 3 4 5 6 7 8 9 10 VH 98 97 96 95 94

ACKNOWLEDGMENTS ▼

We wish to thank all of those who have made this book possible: Elinor Chamas, Judith Bittinger, Karen Howse, and Evelyn Nelson, for their encouragement and invaluable suggestions; Louisa Hellegers, Debbie Sistino, and Tab Hamlin who made their own very special contributions along the way; Joanne Dresner who believed it could be done; Polli Heyden and Anita Palmer who spent many hours helping us secure permissions; Leslie Jo Adams and Linda Sasser for sharing parts of their personal libraries with us; all of the consultants, reviewers, and fieldtesters who so generously gave their time and expertise at various stages of the project; Mark Hansen who helped us conceptualize some of the illustrations; Jennifer Johnson for her assistance with visual material; and the many authors and artists from whom we drew contributions. In addition, we are very grateful to our families for their love, encouragement, and patience.

Consultants

Jo Fritschel, San Diego City Schools • Virginia Jama, New York City Public Schools • Rubbie Patrick Herring, Memphis City Schools

Reviewers and Fieldtesters

Fanny Freytes • Celeste DeCoudres • Susan Slome
Jean Hernandez • Vivien Wake • Marie Aloise
Luis Raul Mondriquez

TO THE TEACHER ▼

Worlds Together: A Journey into Multicultural Literature reflects the cultural diversity found in our schools and in our communities. It is about people—their joys and sadness, their hopes and dreams, their courage and determination. Through its universal themes, the book promotes positive human values including honesty, love, and kindness, not only toward other people but toward all living things.

The book is intended for adolescent students with emerging language skills either in second language programs or in traditional language arts classes and language development programs. The emphasis is on integrated language skills, including reading, writing, speaking, listening, and thinking, which require students to participate as active learners.

Each theme begins with a Getting Started brainstorming session focused on students' prior knowledge and experience. Their own cultures, goals, and expectations are all explored in relation to the authentic readings presented. Each selection concludes with numerous discussion ideas and a choice of meaningful activities tailored to individual learning styles.

An accompanying Teacher's Resource Book includes reproducible activity masters with additional collaborative activities, performance-based assessment instruments, portfolio suggestions, teacher strategies, and background information on the literature, authors, and artists represented in the book.

It is our goal to help teachers establish reading environments which are both enjoyable and instructive. It is our hope that *Worlds Together* will enable students to find reading an exciting and very personal adventure.

TO THE STUDENT ▼

In *Worlds Together* you will learn about many people. You will share their experiences and their feelings. You will find out how they live and what they think is important. In this book you will meet people who are like you and others who are very different from you. You will see them face problems and find ways to bring happiness into their own lives and into the lives of others.

The activities will help you understand what you read. Through them, you will see what meaning the readings have for you and the others in your class. Sometimes you will work with a partner or in a group. Other times you will work by yourself. The activities will help you improve your skills in reading, writing, speaking, listening, and thinking.

We hope that you will enjoy and learn from this journey into multicultural literature. Let us now begin....

Patricia Richard–Amato
Wendy Abbott Hansen

CONTENTS

UNIT FIVE
Faces of Love

UNIT SIX

Worlds Together

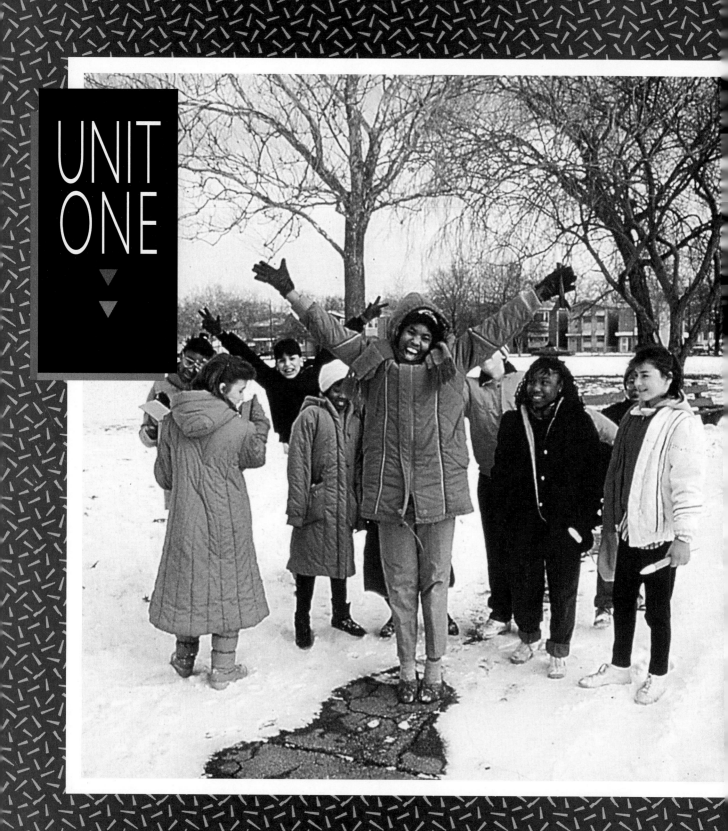

UNIT
ONE
▼
▼

Justo a mi
me toco
ser yo.

Only I
Can be me.

anonymous

A World of My Own

In this unit, you will read about being yourself. You will have a chance to discover some things that are special about you and other people.

▼

Getting Started

talents Activities that people have the ability to do well.

Think about people you know. They are all different in many ways. And you are different from each of them. That's partly because each person has interests and talents that help make that person special. To discover more about your own interests and talents, think about what you enjoy doing the most. Make a list of the things you like to do. See the example below to help you begin.

THINGS I LIKE TO DO

—play my guitar
—go to the movies

Now share your list with a partner. How is your list similar to or like your partner's? How is it different? Use a chart such as the one below to record your ideas.

similarities The ways in which people, places, or things are alike.

COMPARING OUR INTERESTS AND TALENTS

Similarities

Differences

—We both like to read.

—My partner likes to play baseball, but I like to play soccer.

This poem suggests that you are the only one in the world with your thoughts and your dreams. See how the poem makes you feel.

Truly My Own

Vanessa Howard, Age 13

I think if I searched a thousand lands
and twice the number in rainbows,
I'd never find one human being who chose
the things that I chose,
a person who wanted the things I wanted
or sought what I sought to be.

I'd never find one human being
like or compared to me
and if I traveled seven seas
I still would be alone
for there is no one who thinks like me
for my dreams are truly my own.

images Pictures.

sought The past tense of seek which means to look for.

WITH YOUR CLASS ▼

Think about the poem. Discuss it with your class and the teacher. The questions below may help you.

1. How does the poet feel about being different from others? Happy? Sad? How do you know?

2. Do you agree with the poet? Do you think you are like no other person on earth? Why?

3. What might happen to a person who tries to be just like someone else? Is it difficult trying to be like someone else? Why or why not?

One way to discover what makes you different from others is to find out more about some things you and some of your classmates like best. With your partner make up a questionnaire such as the one below. You and your partner may add questions of your own. Fill in the first column. Then interview at least two other classmates and fill in the other columns.

With your partner, talk about differences between your answers and those of your classmates. What are the similarities?

WHAT WE LIKE BEST	Me	Abdul	Maria
Question			
1. What do you like to read about the most?			
2. What is your favorite school subject?			
3. What do you like to do best when you're by yourself?			
4. What is one thing you would like to learn how to do better?			

FOLKTALES are make-believe, sometimes magical stories about kings, queens, princes, gods, goddesses, and so on. They are often told for entertainment. But they are also told to teach important lessons. Can you find a lesson in this story?

Look at the pictures in this story. What do you think the story will be about? Discuss with your class.

▼

This story is a Greek folktale about a princess named Atalanta and her father, the king. Atalanta finds that she and her father do not agree about her future. Can she live life her own way? Or does she have to follow the plan her father has for her?

ATALANTA

Betty Miles

ONCE UPON A TIME, not long ago, there lived a princess named Atalanta, who could run as fast as the wind.

She was so bright, and so clever, and could build things and fix things so wonderfully, that many young men wished to marry her.

"What shall I do?" said Atalanta's father, who was a powerful king. "So many young men want to marry you, and I don't know how to choose."

"You don't have to choose, Father," Atalanta said. "I will choose. And I'm not sure that I will choose to marry anyone at all."

"Of course you will," said the king. "Everybody gets married. It is what people do."

"But," Atalanta told him, with a toss of her head, "I intend to go out and see the world. When I come home, perhaps I will marry and perhaps I will not."

The king did not like this at all. He was a very ordinary king; that is, he was powerful and used to having his own way. So he did not answer Atalanta, but simply told her, "I have decided how to choose the young man you will marry.

toss of her head A movement that involves turning the head back quickly and bringing it forward again.

intend Plan to.

ordinary Common, not different or unusual.

I will hold a great race, and the winner—the swiftest, fleetest young man of all—will win the right to marry you."

Now Atalanta was a clever girl as well as a swift runner. She saw the she might win both the argument and the race—provided that she herself could run in the race, too. "Very well," she said, "But you must let me race along with the others. If I am not the winner, I will accept the wishes of the young man who is."

The king agreed to this. He was pleased. He would have his way, marry off his daughter, and enjoy a fine day of racing as well. So he directed his messengers to travel throughout the kingdom announcing the race with its wonderful prize: the chance to marry the bright Atalanta.

As the day of the race drew near, flags were raised in the streets of the town, and banners were hung near the grassy field where the race would be run. Baskets of ripe plums and peaches, wheels of cheese, ropes of sausages and onions, and loaves of crusty bread were gathered for the crowds.

Meanwhile, Atalanta herself was preparing for the race. Each day at dawn, dressed in soft green trousers and a shirt of yellow silk, she went to the field in secret and ran across it—slowly at first, then faster and faster, until she could run the course more quickly than anyone had ever run it before.

As the day of the race grew nearer, young men began to crowd into the town. Each was sure he could win the prize, except for one; that was Young John, who lived in the town. He saw Atalanta day by day as she bought nails and wood to make a pigeon house, or chose parts for her telescope, or laughed with her friends. Young John saw the princess only from a distance, but near enough to know how bright and clever she was. He wished very much to race with her, to win, and to earn the right to talk with her and become her friend.

"For surely," he said to himself, "it is not right for Atalanta's father to give her away to the winner of the race.

swiftest Having the greatest speed.

fleetest An old-fashioned word meaning fastest.

argument A discussion where there is disagreement.

kingdom The land controlled by the king.

announcing Making known; spreading the news.

bright Here it means smart; intelligent.

banners Long pieces of cloth with decorations or words on them.

preparing Getting ready.

trousers Long pants that are usually worn by men.

course The path followed by the runners.

pigeon A common bird.

telescope A scientific instrument for making objects appear larger and nearer.

Atalanta herself must choose the person she wants to marry, or whether she wishes to marry at all. Still, if I could only win the race, I would be free to speak to her, and to ask for her friendship."

Each evening, after his studies of the stars and the seas, Young John went to the field in secret and practiced running across it. Night after night, he ran fast as the wind across the twilight field, until he could cross it more quickly than anyone had ever crossed it before.

At last, the day of the race arrived.

Trumpets sounded in the early morning. The young men gathered at the edge of the field, along with Atalanta herself. She was the prize they sought. The king and his friends sat

twilight The faint light just after sunset.

trumpets Musical instruments made of metal tubes with bell-shaped ends. Music is made by blowing into them.

in soft chairs, and the townspeople stood along the course.

The king rose to address them all. "Good day," he said to the crowds. "Good luck," he said to the young men. To Atalanta he said, "Good-bye. I must tell you farewell, for tomorrow you will be married."

"I am not so sure of that, Father," Atalanta answered. She was dressed for the race in trousers of crimson and a shirt of silk as blue as the sky, and she laughed as she looked up and down the line of young men.

"Not one of them," she said to herself, "can win the race, for I will run fast as the wind and leave them all behind."

And now a bugle sounded, a flag was dropped, and the runners were off!

address Give a speech to.

farewell An old-fashioned word for good-bye.

crimson Dark red.

bugle A musical instrument like a trumpet but shorter and more simple.

The crowds cheered as the young men and Atalanta began to race across the field. At first they ran as a group, but Atalanta soon pulled ahead, with three of the young men close after her. As they neared the halfway point, one young man put on a great burst of speed and seemed to pull ahead for an instant, but then he gasped and fell back. Atalanta shot on.

Soon another young man, tense with the effort, drew near to Atalanta. He reached out as though to touch her sleeve, stumbled for an instant, and lost speed. Atalanta smiled as she ran on. I have almost won, she thought.

But then another young man came near. This was Young John, running like the wind, as steadily and as swiftly as Atalanta herself. Atalanta felt his closeness, and in a sudden burst she dashed ahead.

Young John might have given up at this, but he never stopped running. Nothing at all, thought he, will keep me from winning the chance to speak with Atalanta. And on he ran, swift as the wind, until he ran as her equal, side by side with her, toward the golden ribbon that marked the race's end. Atalanta raced even faster to pull ahead, but Young John was a strong match for her. Smiling with the pleasure of the race, Atalanta and Young John reached the finish line together, and together they broke through the golden ribbon.

Trumpets blew. The crowd shouted and leaped about. The king rose. "Who is that young man?" he asked.

"It is Young John from the town," the people told him.

"Very well. Young John," said the king, as John and Atalanta stood before him, exhausted and jubilant from their efforts. "You have not won the race, but you have come closer to winning than any man here. And so I give you the prize that was promised—the right to marry my daughter."

Young John smiled at Atalanta, and she smiled back. "Thank you, sir," said John to the king, "but I could not

put on Here it means to take on.

burst Sudden movement full of force.

pull ahead Run out in front.

gasped Quickly took in a short breath of air.

shot on Moved forward with great speed.

tense With muscles tightly stretched.

stumbled Tripped and almost fell.

steadily Evenly, without tripping.

dashed Moved quickly.

match An equal. Here it means a person who can run as fast as she can. The next sentence is a clue.

exhausted Very tired.

jubilant Very happy.

possibly marry your daughter unless she wished to marry me. I have run this race for the chance to talk with Atalanta, and, if she is willing, I am ready to claim my prize."

Atalanta laughed with pleasure. "And I," she said to John, "could not possibly marry before I have seen the world. But I would like nothing better than to spend the afternoon with you."

Then the two of them sat and talked on the grassy field, as the crowds went away. They ate bread and cheese and purple plums. Atalanta told John about her telescopes and her pigeons, and John told Atalanta about his globes and his studies of geography. At the end of the day, they were friends.

On the next day, John sailed off to discover new lands. And Atalanta set off to visit the great cities.

By this time, each of them has had wonderful adventures, and seen marvelous sights. Perhaps some day they will be married, and perhaps they will not. In any case, they are friends. And it is certain that they are both living happily ever after.

globes Round maps shaped like the world.

geography The study of the earth.

marvelous Great.

WITH YOUR CLASS ▼

Think about the story. Discuss it with your class and the teacher. Use the questions below to help you.

1. Describe Atalanta. Make a list of her interests and talents.

2. What was the king's plan for Atalanta?

3. What did Atalanta want for herself? How did she change the king's plan?

4. How did Atalanta prepare for the race? Why do you think she got ready for the race in secret?

5. Why do you think Young John did not accept the prize the king gave him?

6. Why do you think Young John and Atalanta became friends? In what ways are they alike?

7. Do you think there is a lesson to be learned from this story? If so, what do you think it is?

WITH A SMALL GROUP ▼

Think about the questions below. Talk about two or more questions with a small group.

1. In some cultures, the parents choose which person their child will marry. Often, the marriage partners do not meet each other until right before the wedding day. What do you think about this way of choosing a marriage partner? What are the good things about it? What might be the bad things about it? What do you think is the best way to choose someone to marry?

2. Atalanta says, "I'm not sure that I will marry anyone at all" (page 7). What do you think her life would be like if she did not marry? Do you think this would be a good choice for a woman? What about for a man? Explain your answer to the group.

3. Do you think that you will marry someday? Take a vote in your group. How many students think they will marry? Explain to your group why you voted the way you did.

4. Atalanta did not do as her father wished, at least not right away. Do you think she was right in disagreeing with her father? How important do you think it is for young people to live their lives their own way? How important is it for them to do as their parents wish? Will the age of the young person make a difference? Is it possible for the young person and the parents to reach an agreement?

WITH A PARTNER ▼

Think about your own future. With a partner, discuss your dreams for your life. On your paper, make a cluster such as the one below.

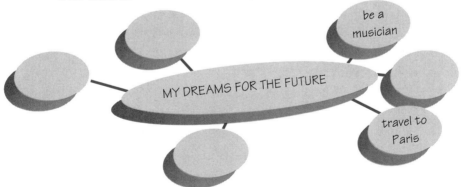

MY DREAMS FOR THE FUTURE

be a musician

travel to Paris

Do you think your parents or guardians will disagree with any of your dreams? If so, which dreams? Will you try to get them to see your point of view? Discuss with your partner.

A journal is a written record of a person's thoughts, experiences, feelings, and dreams. Begin your own journal. You can use a notebook or tablet for this purpose. Your teacher may want you to write in it from time to time. Make sure you enter the date and the topic you are writing about each time you write in your journal.

Your first journal assignment is to write a paragraph about one of the dreams from your cluster (see page 15). Describe your dream. What will you have to do to make it come true? See the example below.

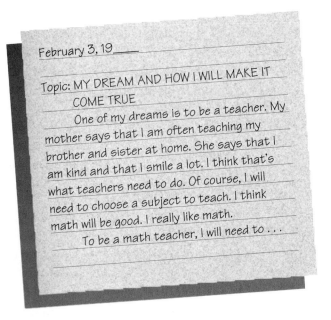

February 3, 19____

Topic: MY DREAM AND HOW I WILL MAKE IT
        COME TRUE
    One of my dreams is to be a teacher. My mother says that I am often teaching my brother and sister at home. She says that I am kind and that I smile a lot. I think that's what teachers need to do. Of course, I will need to choose a subject to teach. I think math will be good. I really like math.
    To be a math teacher, I will need to . . .

If you want, you can share your paragraph with a partner. Ask your partner the questions below about your dream.

a. What is my dream?
b. How will I make it come true?
c. What else can I do to make it come true?

Try one or both of the following activities.

1. Pretend you are Atalanta. Write a letter to your father, the king (see the letter form to the right). In your letter, explain why you made the choice not to marry at this time. Try to get him to agree with you. Ask a partner to pretend to be the king and answer the letter.

June 8, 1999

Dear Father, _____

_____

_____

_____

_____

With love,
Atalanta

2. Write a new ending to the story about Atalanta and Young John. Tell what happens after the race. Describe the adventures each of them has. Tell whether or not they get married. Share your ending with a small group.

THE FOLKTALE

Earlier in this unit you learned that a folktale is a make-believe, sometimes magical story. You learned also that it is often used to teach an important lesson.

1. Do you remember a folktale from the culture you know best? If so, share it with a small group. After you have told the story, talk with your group about what it teaches.

2. Write your own folktale with you as a prince or princess. Include a disagreement with your father, the king, or with your mother, the queen. Many folktales begin with, "Once upon a time . . . . You may want to begin yours this way too.

Once upon a time, _____

_____

_____

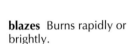
This poem expresses or tells one person's feelings about living life her own way. Does it describe the way you feel? See what you think.

THE SUN AND THE MOON

Elaine Laron

blazes Burns rapidly or brightly.

reflects Mirrors or gives back an image.

bold Striking to the eye. Sometimes means courageous.

The Sun is filled with shining light
It blazes far and wide
The Moon reflects the sunlight back
But has no light inside.

I think I'd rather be the Sun
That shines so bold and bright
Than be the Moon, that only glows
With someone else's light.

WITH YOUR CLASS ▼

Think about the poem. Discuss it with your class and the teacher. Use the questions below to help you.

1. How does the poet describe the sun? The moon?

2. Why do you think the poet says, "I'd rather be the Sun"? Which would you rather be?

LYRIC POETRY ▼

Lyric poems are usually short poems that tell about feelings or ideas. Often they are written in the first person, "I." "The Sun and the Moon" is an example of a lyric poem. What feeling or idea is the author expressing? Discuss with your class and the teacher.

Now try to write your own lyric poem. Write four or more lines describing a feeling or idea that you have. Make yourself the "I" in the poem. Here are some suggestions: the feeling you have when the bell rings at the end of the school day, the happiest moment of your life, what seeing a sunset (or a tree, or a mountain) makes you think of, and so forth.

*W*E KNOW that Atalanta was bright and clever. These were two of her special qualities. Now think about one of your friends or someone close to you. What special qualities does that person have? What do you like about that person? Share your thoughts with a partner.

"True Colors" is a song about valuing a person's special qualities. It shows how a knowledge of these qualities can help people in times of sadness.

True Colors

Billy Steinberg and Denise Barry

discouraged Without hope or courage.

chorus Several lines that are repeated in a song.

bear Cope with or put up with.

You with the sad heart,
Don't be discouraged, I realize
It's hard to take courage
In a world full of people,
You can lose sight of it all,
And the darkness down inside you
Makes you feel so small.

Chorus

But I see your true colors
Shining through.
I see your true colors,
And that's why I love you.
So don't be afraid to let them show.
Your true colors,
True colors are beautiful
Like a rainbow.
Show me a smile then.
Don't be unhappy, can't remember when,
I last saw you laughing.
If this world makes you crazy
And you've taken all you can bear,
Just call me up,
Because you know I'll be there.

(Repeat chorus)

Hoo . . . hoo . . .
Can't remember when I last saw you there

If this world makes you crazy
And you've taken all you can bear,
Just call me up,
Because you know I'll be there.

(Repeat chorus)

WITH YOUR CLASS ▼

Think about the song. Discuss it with your class and the teacher. Use the questions below to help you.

1. Describe the person with the "sad heart" in the song. What problems do you think this person has? What does the singer tell this friend to do? Do you think these suggestions are helpful ones?

2. What are "true colors"? Do you think the word "rainbow" fits here? Why or why not?

3. Do you think the singer of this song is a good friend? Would you like to have a friend like the singer? Tell why.

WITH A PARTNER ▼

Discuss these questions with a partner.

1. What do you do when your friends are sad like the friend in the song? Do you let them know that you like them just the way they are? Think of the people in your life who like you just the way you are. Who are they? Friends? Family? How do you feel when you are with them?

2. Why is it important to let your own true colors shine through? What might happen if you do not?

Try one or both of the following activities.

1. Make a list of your own "true colors," or the qualities that make you who you are. Draw a rainbow using a different color for each quality you have listed. Write the name of the quality on each color. You may want to share your rainbow with at least one other person.

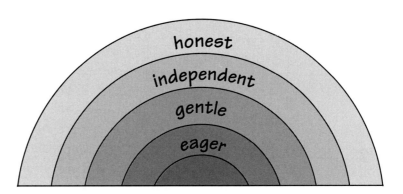

2. Interview family members or friends about your own "true colors." Ask them what they feel your true colors are. Write down what they say. You may want to write what they say in your journal. If you made a rainbow, you may want to add other colors to it based on what other people say about you.

IDEA BOX

DEVELOPING YOUR WORD BANK

One way to help you learn new words is to make a word bank. Write the words you want to learn in a notebook or on index cards (one card for each word or phrase). If you use a notebook, leave plenty of space after each word or phrase. You may work with a partner or have your teacher help you. Beside each word or phrase, write what it means. Then write the word or phrase in a sentence. Drawing a picture may help you remember the meaning. See the examples below. Review your words for a few minutes each day. Ask your teacher or a partner to quiz you on your words from time to time.

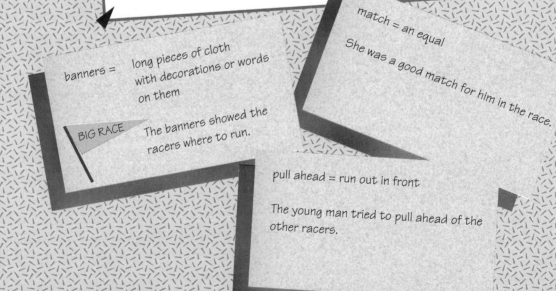

banners =   long pieces of cloth with decorations or words on them

BIG RACE   The banners showed the racers where to run.

match = an equal

She was a good match for him in the race.

pull ahead = run out in front

The young man tried to pull ahead of the other racers.

Making a Collage

Like Atalanta, you, too, have probably discovered that you have special interests and talents. Look through magazines and newspapers and cut out pictures that show your interests and talents. For example, if you play baseball, you might cut out a picture of a person playing baseball. Once you have all your pictures cut out, glue them together on a large piece of paper to make a collage or collection. Talk about your collage with a small group. Tell why you chose these pictures. Your teacher may want you to display your collage in the classroom.

Acting Out

The story about Atalanta came from a Greek legend. Go to your library to see if you can find this Greek legend. You may want your teacher or the librarian to help you. You and your classmates may want to act out the story.

Pen Pals

Pretend you are writing to someone you have never met before. Describe yourself: what you look like, your family, your interests and talents, what you think is important, and so forth. You may use the letter form on page 17 and begin with "Dear Pen Pal."

A follow-up might be to write to a real pen pal. Your teacher might want to pair you up with someone in another class or in another school.

Making Friends in a New World

What is it like to be away from home and in a new world? It may be a new school, a new neighborhood, a new city, or a new country. Are friends easy to find in a new world? In this unit you will read about others' experiences in unfamiliar places. Perhaps you will want to share a few of your own.

▼

Getting Started

Are you now facing a new world—perhaps even a new language and new ways of doing things? If not, imagine that you are. What are some of the problems? Are there any benefits or good things about facing a new world? Discuss with your class. Make a list of possible problems and benefits using the sample chart below to get you started.

PROBLEMS	BENEFITS
—missing old friends	—making new friends

Living in a new world

Facing a new world can make you feel lonely. What is it like to feel lonely? This poem gives one person's answer to that question.

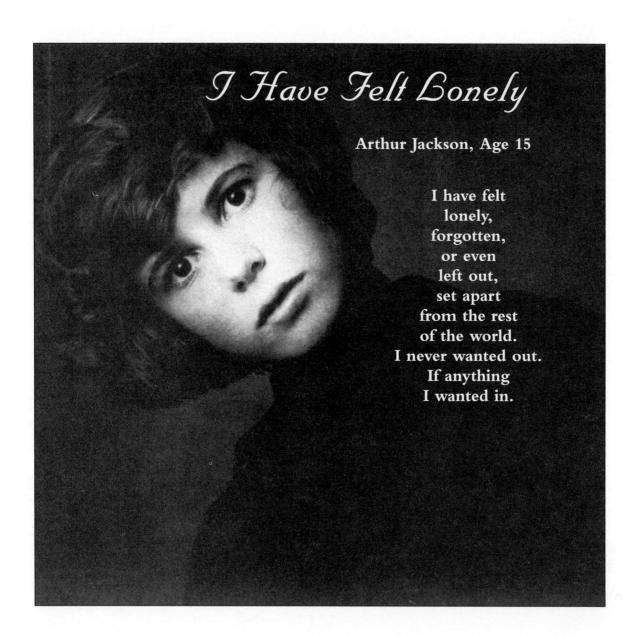

I Have Felt Lonely

Arthur Jackson, Age 15

I have felt
lonely,
forgotten,
or even
left out,
set apart
from the rest
of the world.
I never wanted out.
If anything
I wanted in.

WITH YOUR CLASS ▼

Think about the poem. Talk about it with your class and the teacher. The questions below may help you.

1. Why do you think the poet feels the way he does?

2. What does the poet want? Do you think he will get what he wants? If so, how?

WITH A PARTNER ▼

Discuss these questions with a partner.

The poet says he felt "left out" and "set apart." Have you ever felt that way? Or do you know someone who feels that way? What do you think caused the feeling? How can we help such a person feel better?

Try one or both of these activities.

1. Find a picture of someone who looks lonely. Show the picture to a small group. Discuss with the group why you think that person is lonely. What advice do they have for the person in your picture?

2. Read the poem "I Have Felt Lonely" again. Draw a picture of what comes to your mind. Use color to express what it is like to be lonely. Discuss your picture with a partner. Talk about what is happening in your picture and why you chose the colors you did.

*In the cartoon below, some advice is given
to a person who is lonely.
See what the advice is.*

The Doctor Is In

Charles M. Schulz

WITH YOUR CLASS ▼

Think about the cartoon. Discuss the questions below with your class and the teacher.

1. What advice does the "doctor" in the cartoon give? Do you think the advice is good? Why or why not? Do you think it's easy to follow that advice?

2. Do you think this cartoon is funny? Why or why not?

WITH A PARTNER ▼

It's easy to say, "Get some friends!" But how does a person do this? Making friends may be very hard if you are in a strange place. With your partner, think of some ways to make friends. On your paper make a cluster of your ideas like the one on this page. When you are finished, work with another pair of classmates, and share the ideas you wrote. You may want to add some of the new ones you hear about to your cluster.

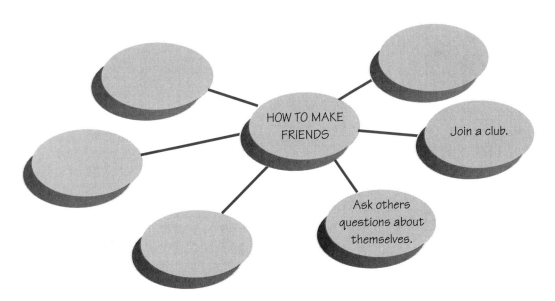

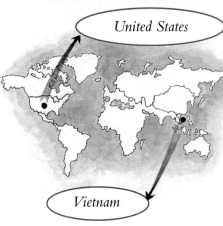

United States

Vietnam

Sometimes embarrassing things happen to us. We may say the wrong thing or do something that only close friends would understand. A very embarrassing thing happened to San Ho at school. He had just arrived in the United States from Vietnam. He had come to live with his mother and her American husband named Stephen. San Ho thought he had left the Vietnam War behind. But was this true?

from

MY NAME IS SAN HO

Jayne Pettit

HOW DIFFERENT everything seemed to me during those first weeks in America with my mother and Stephen. I was very tired at first. The days were long. Not being able to speak English frustrated me. It was hard to concentrate and to keep up with the others as we moved from classroom to classroom.

Then, one day it happened. Throughout the morning, the rain pounded on our windows. The thunder roared. Lightning struck several times, sending blue-white streaks across the dark skies. More than once, a girl with long blonde hair approached my teacher as she moved from one project table to another. The girl said nothing. My teacher smiled, said something to her in a whispered voice, and patted her gently on the arm. One of the boys in the class laughed and poked the boy next to him. I couldn't understand what he said. I have the feeling the boy was making

embarrassing Making a person feel uncomfortable inside.

frustrated Kept from reaching a goal.

concentrate To give careful attention.

blonde Light in color.

approached Came toward.

project A planned activity.

fun of the girl because she was afraid of the lightning. I felt sorry for her. I knew what it was like to be laughed at.

The air was hot and damp as we entered the gym. My hair clung to the back of my neck. My shirt was soaked with sweat. I followed the friendly boy in my group as he walked to one of the tables. Taking out my lunch, I spread it on the table before me. I looked around for my teacher. She always brought her lunch to our table. She would sit down next to me. She would speak to me in short phrases to help me understand what everyone was saying. It was like an informal lesson in speaking my new language. I had come to look forward to this.

making fun of Saying unkind things that cause others to laugh.

clung Stuck to; the past tense of cling, which means to hold on to something tightly.

phrases A small group of words used together to mean something.

informal Not formal or following usual actions.

Seeing my teacher at the doorway, I made room for her on our bench as she approached our table. She motioned to the tall young man who stood near us to join us. I recognized the man as our music teacher. She indicated that he was to sit next to me. Leaning down close to me, she put a hand on my arm and smiled. Then, pointing to the door once more, she said something quickly to the other teacher and walked away from our table. A moment later, she was gone.

A sinking feeling swept through me. I stared at the door, hoping that my teacher would return.

The noise in the room increased as the students came to the end of their meal. Outside, the rain beat down on the high windows along the wall. Thunder cracked. More than once the lights blinked and dimmed. The crowd of students scraped the benches against the floor as they tossed their lunch wrappers into trash bins. Even in the crowd, I felt afraid and alone. Where was my teacher? Why had she left?

motioned Directed by using movements of the body.

indicated Suggested an action with words or movements of the body.

cracked Here is means made a loud noise like something breaking apart.

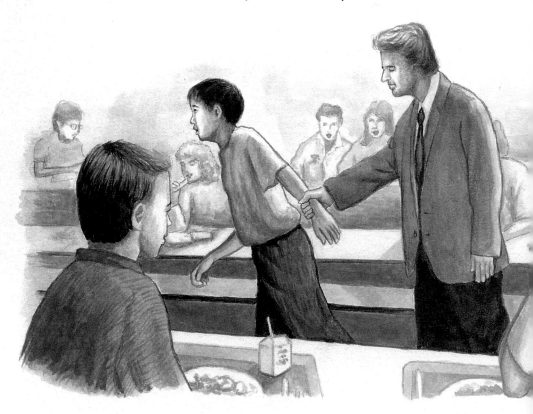

Suddenly, I heard the sound of a siren. It began as a low moan and then rose. Slowly and familiarly it became louder. It filled the air outside with its horrible, screeching wail. Up and down the siren raced. I stared first at one and then another of the students. Why wasn't anyone listening? Why weren't we running toward the door? Where could we hide before it was too late?

I screamed and stood up, tugging at the bench beneath me. I bumped against the teacher sitting alongside of me. The teacher grabbed my arm to steady me. I pulled away. My ears rang with a mournful wail of the siren as it rose and fell. The students' voices stilled, and I heard only the loud claps of thunder and the noise of the siren. The eyes of every person in the room were on me. The terror I had known all my life returned.

"Mother!" I shouted in Vietnamese. "Mother, help me!"

Someone from the other side of the room started to

siren A loud horn or whistle sound to give warning.

moan A low sound like a soft cry.

familiarly Well-known, understood.

screeching wail A high, loud cry, often in pain.

tugging Pulling.

mournful wail A cry full of grief or sorrow.

stilled Became quiet.

laugh. Another joined him, and then another and another. It seemed that everyone in the room was laughing at me. I stood there, frozen with fear. My eyes begged the teacher next to me to do something. Why were they laughing at me? Didn't they know they should be running for cover?

The music teacher put his arm across my shoulders. He held me firmly as I tried to wrench away. The students began heading for the door. Their laughter echoed around me as they shoved in front of me. I realized that they didn't know what I knew. They'd never had to run for cover. They'd never seen friends lying on the ground, their bodies stilled by death.

My screams turned to sobs. I called for my mother. Again and again I begged for her to come and take me to a safe place. Through my sobs I strained for the sounds I had been waiting to hear: the quick, darting sounds of jets as they soared above my village; the thump of artillery fire as it shot into the ground above my head. But there were none of these. Only the voices of the students as they hurried to their rooms. The siren outside reached its final pitch. Then it was silent.

I looked up at the teacher. My knees trembled. I knew that if I tried to move I would fall to the floor. I stood there, listening to his calm voice. He spoke softly. I could only guess they were words of comfort. It was then that I noticed the dark-haired boy coming around from his side of the table. He had not laughed at me. Neither had the teacher, nor the girl who had been afraid of the lightning that morning. Together, we all moved to the door. My sobs quieted as we slowly made our way down the long hallway and back to our room. My fear and anger disappeared, only to be replaced by the dreadful embarrassment that swept through me. What must everyone think of me?

wrench away Pull away with force.

echoed Was sent back from the walls; repeated.

shoved Pushed.

sobs Sounds made when crying.

strained Used great effort.

darting Making rapid, sudden movements.

soared Flew upward.

artillery Large guns.

pitch A tone or sound.

trembled Shook.

dreadful Terrible.

The music teacher walked me to the door of my classroom. I went in to see that my teacher had returned. My shoulders slumped and my arms fell limp. I walked to my desk and sank into my seat. The room was silent as I became aware that no one was laughing at me now. No one was threatening me with stares. Had they finally understood? Had someone explained to them the terror that I could not describe? My eyes dropped to the floor. I reached for my pencil and went through the motions of working.

Later my teacher took us to the film room, where we watched a movie about Jacques Cousteau. His group of underwater explorers swam with giant fish through beds of coral. Plants swayed and shimmered in the silence of the sea. The beauty and peace of the film calmed me, and I began to feel better.

At last, it was time to go home.

Later that day, Stephen returned from the naval base. He parked his small red car in the driveway at the side of our house. What will he think, I wondered, when my mother tells him about what happened at school? I looked up from my studies. He leaned down to give my mother a hug. I hoped he would not be angry at me.

My mother explained what had happened to me that day in school. Stephen listened intently. His face grew serious. A frown developed on his forehead. He stood with his hands folded behind his back and then he looked my way. Our eyes met and I wasn't sure of his reaction. I wished that I could leave the room. Finally, Stephen walked over to where I was sitting. He put a hand on my arm and said something to my mother. Then he spoke to me in a quiet, reassuring tone. As he finished my mother translated his words.

"Stephen says there will be no more wars in this country, my son. He says you can count on him and that you can trust his words to be true."

slumped Fell or drooped.

threatening Promising to do harm.

motions Actions.

Jacques Cousteau A French underwater explorer and writer.

coral Pink rocklike structures formed by a small sea animal.

swayed Moved back and forth.

shimmered Gave back light.

naval base Where people in the navy live and work.

intently With full attention.

frown An expression caused by displeasure.

reaction An act in answer to something.

reassuring Calming; causing to feel sure again.

translated Said in another language.

count on him Know that he will do what he promises.

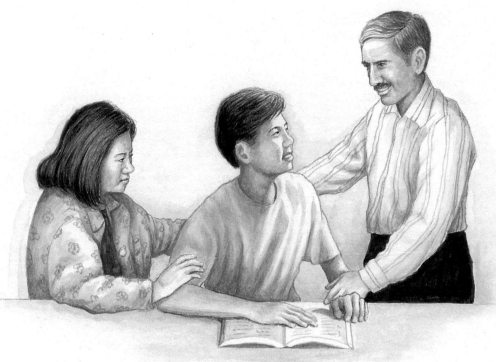

confide Tell private thoughts.

resentful Feeling that someone has harmed you in some way.

Marine A type of soldier who serves both on land and on sea.

I thought of some words my mother said one time about being a friend to someone who needed you. Now those words seemed to apply to Stephen and me. I slowly put down my pencil and looked up into his worried face. He put his other hand on my shoulder as tears fell down my cheeks. Stephen and I were going to be friends. Good friends. Friends who could count on each other, trust each other, and confide in each other. I realized I was no longer afraid or resentful of the young American Marine my mother had married.

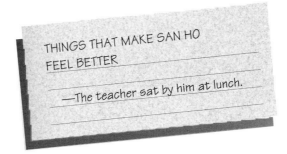

WITH YOUR CLASS ▼

Think about the story. Talk about it with your class and the teacher. The questions below may help you.

1. What are some problems that San Ho had when he first came to America?

2. Why did the students laugh at the blonde girl in San Ho's class?

3. What did San Ho's teacher usually do at lunch? How did this help San Ho?

4. What did San Ho's teacher do today that was different from the other days? How did this difference make San Ho feel?

5. What sound frightened San Ho? Why did the sound frighten him? Where had he heard that sound before? What did it mean in the place where he lived before?

6. Why did the students laugh at San Ho? Did everyone laugh at him? Who didn't? Why didn't they laugh?

7. What did Stephen do when he heard about what happened to San Ho at school? Was San Ho surprised at Stephen's reaction? Why?

8. What kinds of things seemed to make San Ho feel better throughout the story? Make a list.

THINGS THAT MAKE SAN HO
FEEL BETTER

—The teacher sat by him at lunch.

WITH A PARTNER ▼

Discuss one or more of the following questions with a partner.

1. Why do you think San Ho felt alone in the crowd of people in the gym? Have you ever felt alone in a crowd? Why do you think this happens sometimes?

2. Have experiences from your past ever come back to frighten you? What happened? What did you do? How did others react?

3. Our friends are sometimes much older or younger than we are. For example, Stephen, an adult, was San Ho's friend. Have you ever had a friend who was much older or younger than you? Talk about your friend. Why do you think you became friends?

WITH A SMALL GROUP ▼

Think about the questions below. Then share your thoughts with a small group.

1. How does San Ho know that he and Stephen will be good friends? What does it mean to San Ho to be a good friend? Do you agree with him? What does it mean to be a good friend in the culture you know best? List some words that you think describe a good friendship.

2. San Ho was so afraid that he cried in the story. Is it all right to cry? Does the culture you know best encourage or discourage crying? Does age make a difference? Is it different for males and females? If so, why do you think it is different?

THE PLOT OR CHAIN OF EVENTS ▼

A plot or chain of events is all the things that happen in a story. It tells which thing happens first, which one happens second, and so forth. See the sample chain below. Like all chains, it is made of links. Notice that the links are joined together. Each link contains an event that is important to the meaning of the story. The first four links are filled in for you already. Work with a partner to make a similar chain on your paper. Use as many links as you need.

Chain of Events

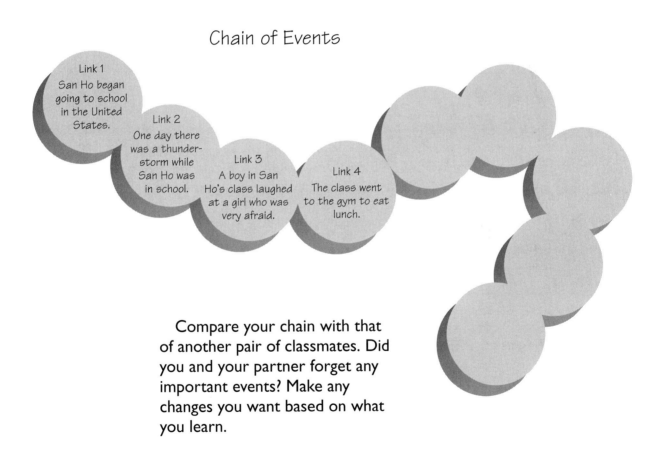

Link 1
San Ho began going to school in the United States.

Link 2
One day there was a thunder-storm while San Ho was in school.

Link 3
A boy in San Ho's class laughed at a girl who was very afraid.

Link 4
The class went to the gym to eat lunch.

Compare your chain with that of another pair of classmates. Did you and your partner forget any important events? Make any changes you want based on what you learn.

POINT OF VIEW ▼

Every story has a point of view. Some "voice" tells the story. Sometimes it is the voice of one of the characters, one of the persons in the story. In this story, San Ho's own voice tells the story. The point of view is San Ho's. Through his point of view, we learn his understanding of what happened.

Now pretend that some other character is telling this story. How will it be different? Do the following activity to see how a story can be different if it is told from the point of view of someone else.

Divide into small groups. Each group should choose one of the following characters: San Ho's mother, a classmate who laughed at San Ho, the blonde girl, San Ho's teacher.

Pretend to be that character. With your group, tell the story from that character's point of view. Use the first person "I" when telling the story. One person in your group should write down the story as the group tells it. For example, a group telling the story from the point of the blonde girl might say things like, "Poor San Ho. I know what it's like to be laughed at. The sky was so dark that day and the thunder was so loud. I was afraid."

When your group is finished with its story, share it with the whole class. See if they can guess whose point of view your group used.

Try the following.

Pretend that you are San Ho's friend. Write a letter to him. In your letter try to help him feel better. Perhaps you can share with him one of your own embarrassing experiences or some of your own problems with being a long way from home. See the letter form on page 17.

IDEA BOX

DEVELOPING YOUR WORD BANK

Continue developing your Work Bank.
See the directions on page 24.

Making a Class Scrapbook

Write a short paragraph about yourself.
Include your name and tell a little bit about your
life and your family. If you are now facing a new
world, talk about what it is like. Include your
experience with making new friends. Your paragraph may begin like this.

My name is . . .
_____
_____

Now show your paragraph to a partner. Ask
your partner to make comments or ask questions about what you say in your paragraph. You
may want your partner to help you rewrite your
paragraph. Then bring to class a photo of yourself and perhaps some of your family members.
Put together a class scrap book to display in
your room.

Learning About Others Through Interview

Interview one or two people who are from another country. You can choose people from your school or community. Write down their responses to your questions. Share some of the more interesting responses with a small group. You may want to use a form such as the one to the right for your interviews.

INTERVIEW

What country did you come from? When did you come?

Why did you come to this country?

What problems did you have when you first came?

What do you like about being in this country?

What advice would you give to someone else who is new to this country?

Helping New Students in Your School

With your class, decide what you can do to help students who are new to your school. You may want to include some of the ideas below.

A. Plan a tour of the school for individuals or small groups of students who speak the same language. If possible, have someone who speaks that language give the tour.

B. Make a guidebook with a map of the school in it. Tell in simple English where certain things can be found and how certain things are done (how to get a lunch ticket, etc.). You may want to include a small dictionary of useful phrases. You may want to say what the English words mean in several languages.

C. Tell at least one new student that you will be his or her friend. Help that student in any way you can. You may want to help with homework, share ideas and experiences, and so forth.

With your group, decide what advice you will give. Have a volunteer in your group write down the situation at the top of a piece of paper. The volunteer should then write the number of the group and the group's advice. Then pass the paper to another group for their advice. The papers will be passed from group to group until every group has had a chance to give advice for each situation. When all have finished, volunteers can read the advice aloud to the class.

Advice for Friends

Divide into small groups. Each group should have a number. With your group choose one of the situations presented here to give advice about. Do not choose one that another group has already chosen. Your group may want to write a situation of its own and use it instead of one of these.

A. Your friend is very upset. He has failed an important exam in his science class. He says he studied hard and read all the assignments. Later he tells you that he sometimes has trouble understanding what the teacher says in class.

B. Your friend has been asked to go to a movie by someone of another ethnic group. He wants to go very much. His parents say that he should not go. They tell him to choose friends only from his own ethnic group.

C. Your friend is frustrated. Her social studies teacher has told her not to speak her own language with her friends at school. The teacher has told her to speak only English if she wants to learn it.

UNIT THREE

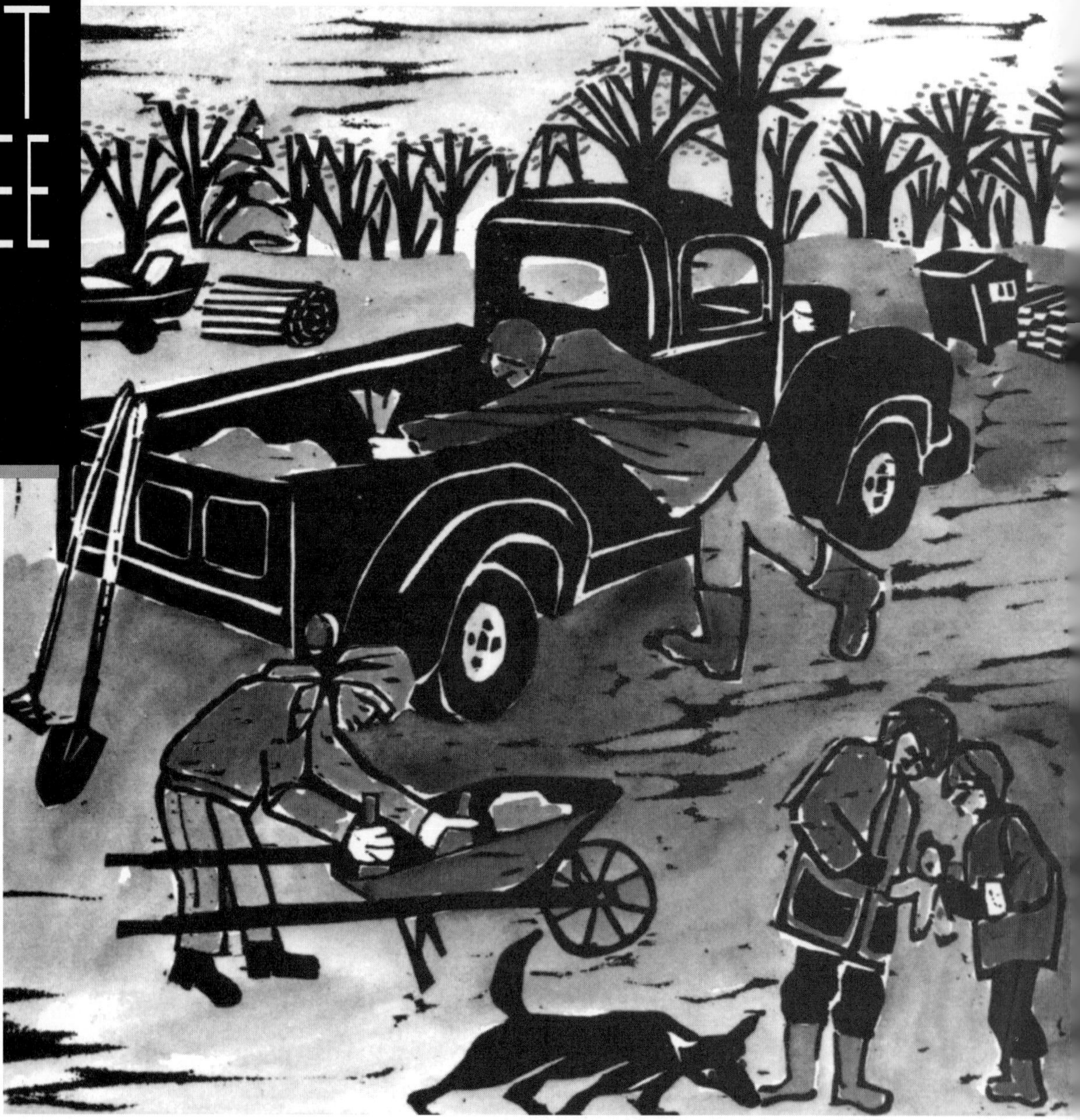

Family Connections

Families are worlds of their own, where people have deep connections to each other. Sometimes these connections are loving or playful and sometimes sorrowful. As you read the unit, think about your own family. What makes your family special? Think about the connections the people in your family have to each other.

▼

Tell about the family you see here in this picture. What are the members of the family doing together? Do you think they are happy? Why or why not?

Getting Started

identity The things that make something different from the others.

Large, small, Asian, African, poor, wealthy, all families have their own identity. They have their own traditions or ways of doing things. They have their own rules, habits and beliefs. These things connect family members together. Make a tree of your own family like the one below. Include the persons who are members of your family. Your tree may have many branches or it may have only two.

Fill in the roots of the tree with the things that connect your family. See the example below.

My Family Connections

Sometimes family members are related. Sometimes they are not. Some members may have been adopted. Some may have come into a family through marriage or as foster children. Some may simply be close friends. The song "Free to Be . . . a Family" celebrates what is special about each family. As you read the words, think of what you like most about your own family.

FREE TO BE . . . A FAMILY

Sarah Durkee and Paul Jacobs

related Connected by blood or marriage.

adopted Belonging legally to a family that one was not born into.

foster children Children taken care of by another family until their own parents can care for them again.

reachin' Reaching.

workin' Working.

solo Alone.

We're all branches of the same big family tree,
but every family's different, don't you know?
Reachin' for the sun comes very naturally.
We've only got to let each other grow!

I've got a home . . .
I've found my place . . .
I live with people who are glad to see my face.

We're free to be . . .
you and me,
and you and me,
we're free to be . . . a family!

We're all workin' in the same big marching band,
but drums and horns have different things to say.
All together we'll ring music through the land
We've only got to let each other play!
I've got a place . . .
I've found my home . . .
I'm only solo when I want to be alone.

We're free to be . . .
you and me,
and you and me,
we're free to be . . . a family!

So many groups in the family soup,
So many combinations,
Might be people who look like you
or they might be no relation!
Birds of a feather, they flock together,
Yes, sometimes they do.
But if a little bird joins an elephant herd,
Hey, that's a family, too!

We're all cookin' up the same big barbecue,
but we like spicy, you like sticky sweet.
Maybe we can trade our recipe with you.
Then how about we help each other eat?!

This is my home . . .
These are my folks . . .
These are our secrets and our habits
and our jokes.

We're free to be . . .
you and me,
and you and me,
we're free to be . . . a family!

combinations Two or more things joined together.

Birds of a feather, they flock together A common saying meaning people who are alike often get together.

herd A group of animals.

cookin' Cooking.

barbecue Meat cooked on an open flame. A sauce is often poured on it for added flavor.

folks Here it means the people one belongs with.

WITH YOUR CLASS ▼

Discuss the song with your class and teacher. The questions below may help you.

1. Discuss what is meant by the words "Reachin' for the sun comes very naturally, we've only got to let each other grow" (page 52). How do families "let each other grow"?

2. Look at the words "But if a little bird joins an elephant herd, Hey that's a family, too" (page 53). What does this say about families? Give examples of different kinds of families.

WITH A PARTNER ▼

Tell your partner a little about each member of your family. Describe each person's likes and dislikes, qualities, and so forth. Tell how they are different from each other.

Try the following activities.

1. Often what connects family members are the activities the family does together. Use a box such as the one below to list your own family activities. Share your list with a partner.

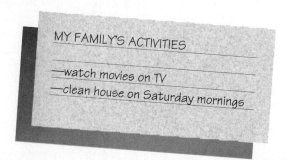

MY FAMILY'S ACTIVITIES

—watch movies on TV
—clean house on Saturday mornings

2. Families are often connected through their traditions. Traditions are ways of doing things, often at special times of the year.

Make a cluster such as the one below to write your own family's traditions. Share your cluster with a small group.

MY FAMILY'S TRADITIONS

going to a favorite restaurant on birthdays

Looking at Literature

Using Comparison

We already learned that when we compare things, we show how they are similar. Authors often use comparisons to make their meaning clearer to the reader. In the song you just read, the family and its members are compared to many things. For example, look again at the line "But if a little bird joins an elephant herd, Hey that's a family, too." We discovered here that you can join a family, even one that is very different from you.

Discuss the following lines from the song with your class and the teacher. How does each comparison help to make clear what it means to be a family?

"We're all branches of the same big family tree . . ." (page 52)

"We're all cookin' up the same big barbecue . . . " (page 53)

Find at least one other comparison from the song. Discuss it with your class.

Can you and your class think of any more things to which a family might be compared? Make a list. Explain how each comparison clarifies what it means to be a family.

THE NAVAJOS are a group of American Indians living in the Southwestern United States. Most live in New Mexico, Arizona, and Utah. They are also called the Diné, which means "People of the Earth."

Often our families give us much more than material things like food, clothing, and shelter. They can give us feelings of safety, of being loved. See how the poet in this poem puts into words these feelings that are so difficult to describe.

The Simple Happiness of a Navajo Girl

Ann Clark

My mother's hogan is dry
against the gray mists
of morning.

My mother's hogan is warm
against the gray cold
of morning.

I sit in the middle
of its rounded walls,
walls that my father built
of juniper and good earth.

Walls that my father blessed.
with song and corn pollen.

Here in the middle
of my mother's hogan
I sit
because I am happy.

hogan A rounded Navajo house made of earth and wood.

mists Fine rains made up of very small drops of water.

juniper A green bush.

blessed Made holy.

pollen Powderlike dust given off by the male part of a plant.

WITH YOUR CLASS

Discuss the poem with your class and the teacher. The questions below may help you.

1. Describe the hogan in the poem. Why do you think the hogan means so much to the Navajo girl?

2. Why do you think the poet calls her happiness a "simple" happiness in the title of the poem? What other feelings besides happiness could she be feeling?

Try one of the following activities.

1. Reread the poem. Draw a picture of what comes into your mind. It may be a picture of a Navajo girl in her hogan or of your own home. Or it may be of something else. You and your class may want to display your drawings with the poem in your classroom.

2. Make a floor plan of your own home and put a circle around your favorite room. Share with a small group. Describe your favorite room and why you like it. Tell how this special place makes you feel.

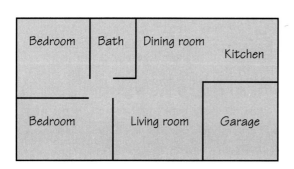

stepfather The husband of one's mother by a later marriage.

start me off Have me begin or get me going.

step-daughter (stepdaughter) a daughter by marriage.

delighted Very happy.

"Twanna and Me" is a true story about an eight-year-old girl and her stepfather. Twanna becomes her stepfather's teacher. Read to see why she does this and how her family becomes closer because of it.

Twanna and Me

Orlando Perez

MY DAUGHTER, Twanna, helps me to read, and she is only eight years old. She is very smart in all her work and she reads most of the time. When she teaches me, she corrects me when I am wrong. She chooses some of the books from her school, and some from home.

After supper she says, "Okay, Perez, let's read." The first thing she does is to start me off. Then she says, "Now you go." And she pushes me to read because she wants me to learn.

Twanna is only my step-daughter and at first we had a rough time to get along. She thought I was taking her mother away from her. But she understands now that her mother needs a husband and she needs a father.

Her mother said, "Twanna, do you want to help Perez to read?" "Yes, Mom, I'll show him," she said. "I'll be his teacher." Sometimes I tell her, "Now I know how to read." She says, "No you don't. I'm still your teacher."

When Orlando Perez finished writing this piece, he showed it to Twanna. She was delighted and asked to take it to school, where she read it to her entire class.

WITH YOUR CLASS

Think about the story. Discuss it with your class and the teacher. The questions below may help you.

1. What does Twanna teach Orlando to do? List the things she does as a teacher.

2. How did Twanna and Orlando get along at first? How do they get along now? Why do you think their relationship changed?

3. Like Twanna and Orlando, sometimes children and adults exchange roles. For example, the adult may become like the child and the child like the adult. Twanna has a skill that Orlando wanted to learn. Discuss other examples of times when children and adults exchange roles.

Write a paragraph about a family member who taught you how to do something (a skill). You may want to use the topic "(the family member's name) and Me." The skill could be sewing, drawing, building, cooking, a sport, etc. Describe how that person taught the skill to you. What problems did you have with learning that skill? How did the family member help you overcome the problems? You may want to include a photo or drawing.

Make sure you place the date by your entry and write down the topic (see the example on page 16).

If you want, you can share your paragraph with a partner. Ask your partner the questions below after your partner has read your paragraph.

   a. What family member taught me a skill? What skill was it?
   b. How did that person teach me the skill?
   c. What problems did I have?
   d. How did I overcome the problems?

This excerpt from the play I Remember Mama *tells the story of a Norwegian-American family in San Francisco, California, around the year 1910. It tells how a young girl, Katrin, grows up in a large family with more love than money. Find out what lesson Katrin learns from her family about giving and receiving.*

You might notice that the characters sometimes speak in a different way from the way you speak. They speak like many other Norwegian-Americans. The language they use is called a dialect.

Katrin's Present

John van Druten

Norwegian-American (pronounced nor-wée-jen) An American who came from Norway or whose relatives came from Norway.

imagination The forming of mental pictures of what is not actually present.

characters Persons in a play, novel, or story.

CHARACTERS

KATRIN, *the main character*
CHRISTINE, *Katrin's sister*
MADELINE, *friend of Katrin*
DOROTHY, *friend of Katrin and Mr. Schiller's daughter*
MAMA, *also called Marta*
PAPA, *also called Lars*
NELS, *Katrin's older brother*
DAGMAR, *Katrin's youngest sister*
JENNY, *Katrin's aunt*
TRINA, *Katrin's aunt*

NARRATOR: As the scene opens, Katrin has just returned home from practicing a part in a play at school. She is discussing with her sister, Christine, the present she wants to receive for her graduation from eighth grade. Katrin wants an expensive dresser set which includes a comb, brush and a mirror that you hold in your hand.

CHRISTINE: Who said you were going to get the dresser set?

KATRIN: Nobody's said so . . . for certain. But I've sort of hinted, and . . .

CHRISTINE: Well, you're not going to get it.

KATRIN: How do you know?

CHRISTINE: Because I know what you *are* getting. I heard Mama tell Aunt Jenny. Aunt Jenny said you were too young to appreciate it.

KATRIN: What is it?

CHRISTINE: Mama's giving you her brooch. Her *solje*.

KATRIN: That old silver thing of Grandmother's? What would I want an old thing like that for?

CHRISTINE: It's an heirloom. Mama thinks a lot if it.

KATRIN: Well, then, she ought to keep it. You don't really mean that's *all* they're going to give me?

CHRISTINE: What more do you want?

KATRIN: I want the dresser set. My goodness, if Mama doesn't realize what's a suitable present . . . why, it's practically the most important time in a girl's life, when she graduates.

CHRISTINE: And you say you're not selfish!

graduation from the eighth grade In the year 1910, graduations were held after the eighth grade as well as after the twelfth. Many students at that time did not continue school after the eighth grade.

expensive Costing a lot of money.

hinted Suggested in a secretive way.

appreciate To value; to be grateful for.

brooch A pin often worn on a woman's blouse or sweater.

solje The Norwegian word for brooch.

heirloom (pronounced air-loom) Something of value belonging to a family for a long time.

suitable Right or appropriate.

KATRIN: It's not selfishness.

CHRISTINE: Well, I don't know what else you'd call it. With Papa not working, we need every penny we can lay our hands on. Even our little bank's empty. But you'll pester Mama into giving you the dresser set somehow. So why talk about it? I'm going home. *(Goes up the steps and through the curtains.)*

(Katrin *stands alone with a stubborn mouth, and then follows* Christine *up the steps.*)

(*After a pause, the curtains open on the kitchen.* Papa, Mama, Nels *and* Dagmar *are at the table with coffee.* Christine *is clearing the dishes.*)

CHRISTINE: I'll just stack the dishes now, Mama. We'll wash them when we come home. (*Carries them out to the pantry, backstage.*)

lay hands on To get or acquire.

pester Bother or annoy.

stubborn Refusing to obey or give in.

pantry A small room off the kitchen where food and dishes are kept.

PAPA: (*holding up a cube of sugar*): Who wants coffee sugar? (*Dips it in his coffee.*) Dagmar? (*Hands it to her.*) Katrin? (*She comes into the room for the sugar.*)

MAMA: You get your coat, Katrin; you need it.

(Katrin *goes out Back Left.*)

DAGMAR: When can we drink real coffee?

PAPA: One day, when you are grown up.

(Jenny and Trina *have come up the porch steps, Left.* Jenny *knocks.*)

MAMA: There are Jenny and Trina. (*Goes to the door.*) Is good. We can start now. (*Opens the door.* Jenny and Trina *come in.*)

JENNY: Well, are you all ready? Is Katrin very excited?

PAPA: (*nodding*): She ate no supper.

(Mama *has started to put on her hat, and to put on* Dagmar's *hat and coat for her.* Christine *comes back.* Papa *gives her a dipped cube of sugar.*)

JENNY: Is that *black* coffee you dipped that sugar in? Lars, you shouldn't. It's not good for them.

PAPA: I know.

(Katrin *returns with her coat.*)

KATRIN: Aunt Jenny, did you see my graduation present? (*Gets it from a chair.* Christine *gives her a disgusted look and goes out.* Katrin *displays the dresser set.*)

JENNY: But I thought . . . Marta, I thought you were going to give her . . .

MAMA: No, you were right, Jenny. She is too young to appreciate that. She like something . . . more modern.

cube of sugar A little square made of sugar.

porch A covered entry way built out from the house.

is good It is good. (Notice that the adult family members in the play often use language that is sometimes more similar to the Norwegian way of speaking.)

disgusted Filled with dislike or disapproval.

displays Shows by holding it up.

JENNY: H'm! Well, it's very pretty, I suppose, but . . . (*Looks up as* Mama *puts on her coat.*) You're not wearing your *solje!*

MAMA: (*quickly*): No. I do not wear it tonight. Come, Trina, we shall be late.

TRINA: Oh, but Peter isn't here yet.

MAMA: Katrin has her costume to put on. He can follow. Or do you like to wait for Peter?

TRINA: I think . . . if you don't mind . . .

MAMA: You can stay with Lars. He does not have to go to his meeting yet.

JENNY: I hope Katrin knows her part.

PAPA: Sure she knows it. *I* know it, too.

TRINA: It's too bad he can't see Katrin's debut as an actress.

MAMA: You will be back before us, Lars?

PAPA (*nodding*): I think the meeting will not last long.

MAMA: Is good. We go now.

(Mama *goes down porch steps with* Jenny *and* Dagmar. Christine *and* Nels *turn from back and follow, waiting outside for* Katrin, *while the others go ahead.* Katrin *puts on her hat and coat and picks up the dresser set.*)

PAPA (*to* Trina): You like a game of checkers while we wait?

TRINA: Oh, I haven't played checkers in years.

PAPA: Then I beat you. (*Rises to get the checker set.*)

KATRIN: Good-bye, Papa.

costume Clothing an actor wears on the stage.

debut (pronounced day-byoo) First time.

checkers A board game played with colored pieces.

PAPA: Good-bye, daughter. I think of you.

KATRIN: I'll see you there, Aunt Trina.

TRINA: Good luck!

PAPA: I'll get the checkers.

(Katrin *goes down the porch steps to join* Christine *and* Nels. Papa *gets the checker set from the dresser, brings it to the table, and sets it up while the next scene is played outside in the street.*)

CHRISTINE (*contemptuously*): Oh, bringing your cheap trash with you to show off?

KATRIN: It's not trash. It's beautiful. You're just jealous.

CHRISTINE: I told you you'd pester Mama into giving it to you.

KATRIN: I didn't. I didn't pester her at all. I just showed it to her in Mr. Schiller's window. . . .

contemptuously With scorn or deep dislike.

cheap trash Something that has little value; inexpensive junk.

CHRISTINE: And made her go and sell her brooch that her very own mother gave her.

KATRIN: What?

NELS: Chris . . . you weren't supposed to tell that!

CHRISTINE: I don't care. I think she ought to know.

KATRIN: Is that true? did Mama—Nels—?

NELS: Well, yes, as a matter of fact, she did. Now, come on.

KATRIN: No, No, I don't believe it. I'm going to ask Papa.

NELS: You haven't time.

KATRIN: I don't care! (*Rushes back to the house and dashes into the kitchen.* Christine *goes off Left, and* Nels *follows her.*) Papa—Papa—Christine says—Papa, did Mama sell her brooch to give me this?

PAPA: Christine should not have told you that.

KATRIN: It's true, then?

PAPA: She did not sell it. She traded it to Mr. Schiller for your present.

KATRIN (*near tears*): Oh, but she shouldn't. . . . I never meant . . .

PAPA: Look, Katrin. You wanted the present. Mama wanted your happiness; she wanted it more than the brooch.

KATRIN: But I never meant her to do that. (*crying*) She *loved* it so. It was all she had of Grandmother's.

PAPA: She always meant it for you, Katrin. And you must not cry. You have your play to act.

KATRIN (*sobbing*): I don't want to act in it now.

PAPA: But you must. Your audience is waiting.

KATRIN (*still sobbing*): I don't care.

PAPA: But you must care. Tonight you are not Katrin any longer. You are an actress. And an actress must act, whatever she is feeling. There is a saying—what is it—. . . The show must go on. So you stop crying, and go and act your play. We talk of this later. Afterwards.

KATRIN (*pulling herself together*): All right, I'll go.

(*Sniffing a good deal, she picks up the dresser set and goes back to the street and off Down Right. Papa and Trina exchange glances and then settle down to their checkers.*)

PAPA: Now we play.

(*The lights fade and the curtains close.*)

(*Stagehands put a small dressing table at Right. Dorothy and Madeline take their places at the table, dressing in costumes for the play.*)

DOROTHY: I'm getting worried about Katrin. If anything's happened to *her* . . .

MADELINE: I'll forget my lines. I know I will. I'll look out and see Miss Forrester sitting there, and forget every single line.

(Katrin *rushes in from Left. She carries the dresser set, places it on the dressing table.*)

MADELINE: We thought you'd had an accident or something.

audience A group gathered to watch a play or other performance.

sniffing Breathing through the nose while crying.

exchange glances Look at each other in a meaningful way.

settle down Become quiet and relaxed.

stagehands People who arrange the scenery and lights in a play.

accident An unexpected event; often an injury.

KATRIN: Dorothy, is your father here tonight?

DOROTHY: He's going to be. Why?

KATRIN: I want to speak to him. (*Pulls off her hat and coat.*) Will you tell him . . . please . . . not to go away without speaking to me? . . .

DOROTHY: What on earth do you want to speak to Father for?

KATRIN: I've got something to say to him. Something to ask him. It's important. *Very* important.

MADELINE: Is that the dresser set? (*Picks it up.*) Can I look at it a minute?

snatching Taking away quickly.

violently With great force.

emotionally With a lot of feeling.

thrusts Pushes with force.

KATRIN (*snatching it from her, violently*): No!

MADELINE: Why, what's the matter? I only wanted to look at it.

KATRIN (*emotionally*): You can't. You're not to touch it. Dorothy, you take it and put it where I can't see it. (*Thrusts it at her.*) Go on. Take it! Take it! Take it!

(*Lights go out.*)

(*Curtains open on the kitchen.* Mama *and* Papa *talking at the table with cups of coffee.*)

MAMA: I am worried about Katrin, Lars. When it was over, I see her talking with Mr. Schiller—and then she goes to take off her costume, and Nels tells me that he will bring her home. But it is long time, and is late for her to be out. And in the play, Lars, she was not good. I have heard her practice it here, and she was good, but tonight, no. It was as if . . . as if she was thinking of something else all the time.

PAPA: I think maybe she was.

MAMA: But what? What can be worrying her?

PAPA: Marta . . . tonight, after you leave, Katrin found out about your brooch.

MAMA: My brooch? But how? Who told her?

PAPA: Christine.

MAMA (*angry*): Why?

PAPA: I do not know.

MAMA (*rising with sternness and calling*): Christine!
(Christine *enters, wiping a dish*.)

CHRISTINE: Were you calling me, Mama?

MAMA: Yes. Christine, did you tell Katrin tonight about my brooch?

CHRISTINE (*frightened but firm*): Yes.

MAMA: Why did you?

CHRISTINE: Because I hated the smug way she was acting over that dresser set.

MAMA: Is not excuse. You make her unhappy. You make her not good in the play.

CHRISTINE: Well, she made *you* unhappy, giving up your brooch for her selfishness.

MAMA: Is not your business. I choose to give my brooch. Is not for you to judge. And you know I do not want you to tell. I am angry with you, Christine.

CHRISTINE: I'm sorry. But I'm not sorry I told. (*Goes back to the pantry with a stubborn face*.)

PAPA: Christine is the stubborn one.

sternness Seriousness, stiffness.

smug Overly satisfied with oneself.

excuse A pretend or made-up reason.

(Nels and Katrin have approached the house outside Left. They stop and look at each other in the lamplight. Katrin looks scared. Then Nels pats her and she goes in, Nels following. Mama looks up into Katrin's face. Katrin turns away, takes off her hat and coat, and takes something from her pocket.)

NELS: What happened at the meeting, Papa?

PAPA: We go back to work tomorrow.

NELS: Gee, that's great. Isn't it, Mama?

MAMA *(absently)*: Yes, it is good.

KATRIN *(coming to Mama)*: Mama . . . here's your brooch. *(Gives it to her.)* I'm sorry I was so bad in the play. I'll go and help Christine with the dishes. *(Turns and goes out.)*

absently Without thinking.

impressed Moved deeply to feelings of respect.

kinda Kind of.

MAMA *(unwrapping the brooch)*: Mr. Schiller give it back to her?

NELS: We went to his house to get it. He didn't want to. He was planning to give it to his wife for her birthday. But Katrin begged and begged him. She even offered to go and work in his store during her vacation if he'd give it back.

PAPA *(impressed)*: So? So!

MAMA: And what did Mr. Schiller say?

NELS: He said it wasn't necessary. But he gave her a job . . . She's going to work for him, afternoons, for three dollars a week.

MAMA: And the dresser set—she gave that back?

NELS: Yes. She was awful upset, Mama. It was kinda hard for her to do. She's a good kid. Well, I'll say good night. I've got be up early.

PAPA: Good night, Nels.

NELS: Good night, Papa. (*Goes out back Left.*)

MAMA: Good night, Nels.

PAPA: Nels is the kind one. (*Starts to refill Mama's cup. She stops him, putting her hand over cup.?* No?

MAMA (*rising*): Katrin! Katrin!

KATRIN (*coming to the door*): Yes, Mama?

MAMA: Come here. (Katrin *comes to her. Mama holds out the brooch.?* You put this on.

KATRIN: No . . . it's yours.

MAMA: It's your graduation present. I put it on for you. (*Pins the brooch on* Katrin's *dress.*)

KATRIN: I'll wear it always. I'll keep it forever.

MAMA: Christine should not have told you.

KATRIN: I'm glad she did. Now.

PAPA: And I'm glad, too. (*Dips a cube of sugar and holds it out to her.*) Katrin?

KATRIN (*shakes her head*): I'm sorry, Papa. I . . . I don't feel like it. (*Moves away and sits on the extra chair, with her back to room.*)

PAPA: So? So? (*Goes to the dresser.*)

MAMA: What you want, Lars?

(*He does not answer but takes a cup and saucer, comes to the table, and pours a cup of coffee, nodding to* Katrin *with his head.* Mama *nods, pleased, then stops his pouring and fills up the cup from the cream pitcher.* Papa *puts in sugar, and moves to* Katrin.)

PAPA: Katrin. (*Holds out the cup. She turns.*)

KATRIN: For me?

PAPA: For our grown-up daughter.

(*Mama nods.* Katrin *takes the cup, lifts it—then her emotion . . comes over her. She thrusts it at* Papa *and rushes from the room.*)

PAPA: Katrin is the dramatic one! Is too bad. Her first cup of coffee, and she does not drink it.

MAMA: It would not have been good for her, so late at night.

PAPA (*smiling*): And you, Marta, are the practical one.

MAMA: You drink the coffee, Lars. We do not want to waste it. (*Pushes it across to him.*)

(*Lights dim. Curtains close.*)

pitcher A container that holds liquids. It has a spout for easy pouring.

dramatic Highly emotional; exciting.

WITH YOUR CLASS ▼

Discuss the play with your class and the teacher. The questions below may help you.

1. What does Katrin want to receive for her graduation present? How does she learn that she may not be receiving this present? What present is she likely to receive?

2. Why doesn't the family have enough money for an expensive graduation present?

3. Why do you think the adults don't want the children to drink real coffee? When does Papa say the children can drink coffee?

4. What present does Mama give Katrin for her graduation? How did Mama pay for this present? Why did she do this?

5. Who tells Katrin the truth about how her present was paid for? Why do you think this person told Katrin? Do you think it was a good idea for Katrin to hear the truth? Why or why not?

6. What kind of meeting do you think Papa is going to attend? How do you know? (See page 64.)

7. What do you think Papa and Trina might be thinking when they exchange glances? (See page 67.)

8. How does Katrin perform in the play? Why do you think she performs this way?

9. Who do you think Miss Forrester is? (See page 67.)

10. What does Katrin do with her present? What good things happen because of her actions? What do you think Katrin has learned about giving and receiving?

11. Why does Papa offer Katrin a cup of coffee at the end of the play? Why do you think Katrin is not able to drink the coffee?

WITH A SMALL GROUP

1. Discuss the family in the play. What connects its members? Look especially at their rules and traditions, activities, qualities, and so forth. With your group, draw a tree similar to the one on page 50. Put the names of family members on the branches and the things that connect the members on the roots, just as you did for your own family.

2. Do you think the family in the play gets along well together? Why or why not? What about the conflict or fight between Katrin and her sister Christine? Do you think it's healthy for family members to disagree strongly? If so, are there times when it might not be healthy? Discuss with your small group.

WITH A PARTNER ▼

Think about the questions below. Discuss one or both with a partner.

1. Many families have rules about what the children and teenagers can and can't do. One of the family rules in the play was that children could not drink coffee. Talk about the rules you have in your own family. Are there rules about chores, watching television and movies, and so forth? Make a list of these family rules on paper. Did you and your partner list similar rules? Compare them. Use a Venn diagram such as the one below for your comparison.

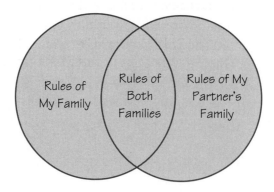

Rules of My Family — Rules of Both Families — Rules of My Partner's Family

2. Papa calls Christine "the stubborn one." Look back through the play. What labels does he have for Nels, Katrin and Mama? Does your family have labels like this for family members? If so, what are they? Does your family have a label for you? Why do you think your family uses it? Tell how you feel about giving labels to family members.

Try one or both of the following activities.

1. Write the name of your own family members on separate index cards. Under the name make a list of presents you think each person would like to receive. Keep these cards in a safe place to help you select presents at a later time.

2. Make a present for someone in your family that shows how you feel about that person. It could be a drawing, poem, photo, or note about how much this person means to you.

In readers' theater, volunteer actors first choose the parts they want to play. They sit or stand in a half-circle in front of the class. Then they read their parts with a lot of feeling. They act out their roles by using their eyes, mouth, and the rest of their bodies, especially their arms, to express emotions. It usually works best if they look at the characters they are speaking to as much as possible while they are reading. One actor, called the narrator, reads the words that tell what the actors do.

Act out "Katrin's Present" in readers' theater. After practicing several times, you and your class may want to present your readers' theater to another class or to invited guests. Or your class might want to videotape the play for future showings.

IDEA BOX

DEVELOPING YOUR WORD BANK

Continue developing your Work Bank.
See the directions on page 24.

Making a Family Album

Collect pictures of your family members. Display these pictures in a photo album or a scrapbook. You may want to tape them to poster board instead. Under each picture, write the family member's name and a few sentences about that person. You may want to tell what the family member does, what that person's qualities are, and so forth. Share your collection with several classmates.

Writing a Short Play

With a small group, write your own short play about a pretend family. Use "Katrin's Present" as a guide. Have a brief speaking role for everyone in your group who wants one. Those who don't want a speaking role can choose to be one of the following:

A The director. The director helps actors with their parts and gives them ideas for how they might move on the stage.

B A stagehand. A stagehand helps set up the stage with chairs, tables, and whatever is needed to suggest a real setting. He or she may also help collect the props (things used by an actor on the stage such as a ball, a pen, a book, etc.).

C A costumer. A costumer finds or makes the clothes or costumes the characters will wear. The costume may only suggest the character. For example, a nurse may wear regular school clothes and only a white nurse's hat made out of paper to suggest that he or she is a nurse.

Each group can present its play for the rest of the class and for any guests who may be invited to the performances. Your class may want to videotape the performance.

Taking a Stand on Family Rules

Family rules are necessary in order for a family to work. Some rules seem fair. Other rules seem unfair or too strict. "Taking a stand" on the fairness of a rule means making a decision about it and then supporting that decision. Think about the following rules.

a. No dating for any family member under fifteen years of age.

b. Teenagers should not be allowed to own cars because they take too much time away from school work.

Working with your whole class, take one rule at a time. Begin with the first rule: No dating for any family member under fifteen years of age. Decide how you feel about that rule and go into one of the following five groups.

1. the group that feels the rule is VERY FAIR
2. the group that feels the rule is SOMEWHAT FAIR
3. the group that is NEUTRAL
   (in other words, they can't decide)
4. the group that feels the rule is SOMEWHAT UNFAIR
5. the group that feels the rule is VERY UNFAIR

Place signs around the room, one for each feeling: VERY FAIR, SOME-WHAT FAIR, NEUTRAL, SOMEWHAT UNFAIR, AND VERY UNFAIR. Go to the sign that best tells how you feel about the rule's fairness. Sometimes there will be only one or two people by a sign.

Once your group is formed, discuss your reasons (or arguments) for feeling as you do about the rule. Choose a group member to be the recorder. This person will write down what the group says.

When the group has finished its discussion (after about four or five minutes), the recorder then will report the group's arguments to the whole class. Even the neutral group can report their reasons for being neutral.

Once all the groups and individuals have reported, then go on to the second rule and do the same thing. You may want to think of other rules for the class to take a stand on. At the end, share with your class how it felt to do this activity.

Writing about a Special Present

Write a paragraph about a present you gave someone in your family that was really appreciated. Describe the gift and why it was special to your family member. How did you feel about giving this present?

Your Family's History

Ask older members of your family about your family's history. Try to discover where your family lived in the early 1900s and before, if possible. Find out as much as you can about where they lived and how they lived. Write the history of your family. You might want to include copies of photos with your history. You and your class might want to put your histories into a book to share with others.

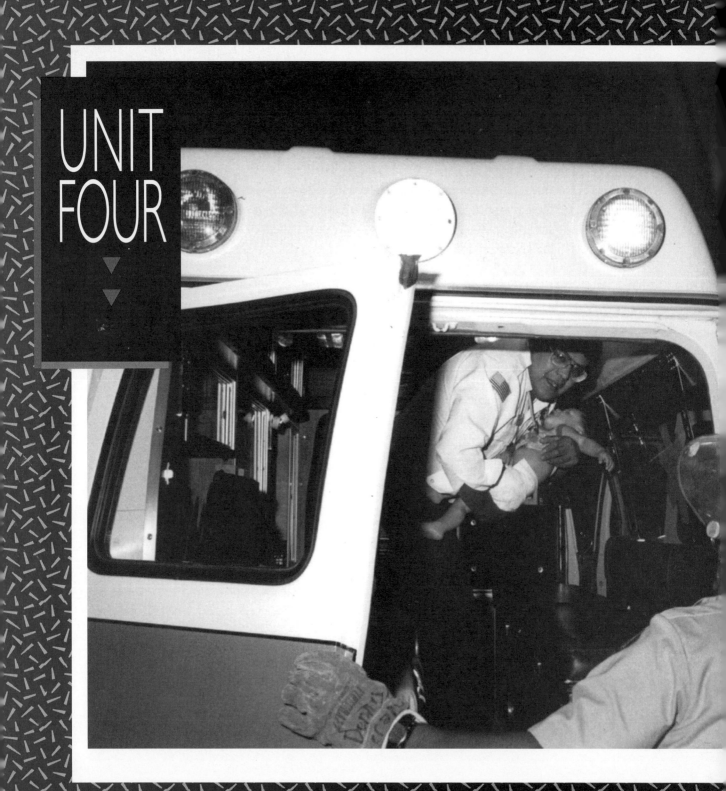

UNIT
FOUR
▼
▼

What Makes a Hero?

This unit is about heroes—how heroes are made and where they can be found. You may not have to look far. Some heroes may be where you would least expect to find them. Maybe you know a few heroes yourself.

▼

What do you think has happened here? Do you think there might be some heroes in this picture? Explain.

What do you think it means to be a hero? Perhaps a hero is someone who is unusually brave or has uncommon strength or speed. With your class, name people you think are heroes. They may be famous people (past or present). They may be people you know in your own neighborhood. They may even be make-believe people in movies you have seen or in stories or cartoons you have read. Think about what it is that makes them heroes. With your class make a cluster such as the one on the next page. Display it in the classroom. You and your classmates may want to add heroes to your cluster after reading this unit.

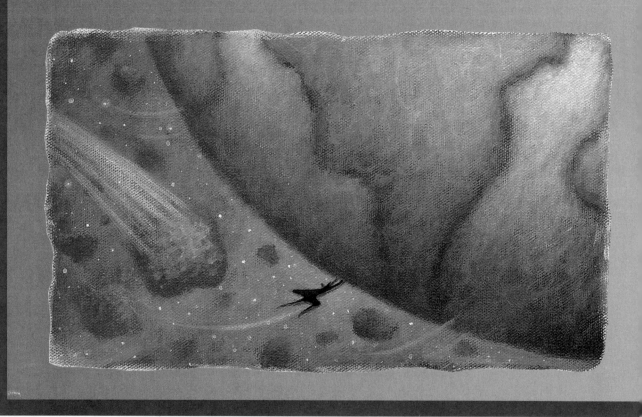

THE HEROES WE KNOW ABOUT

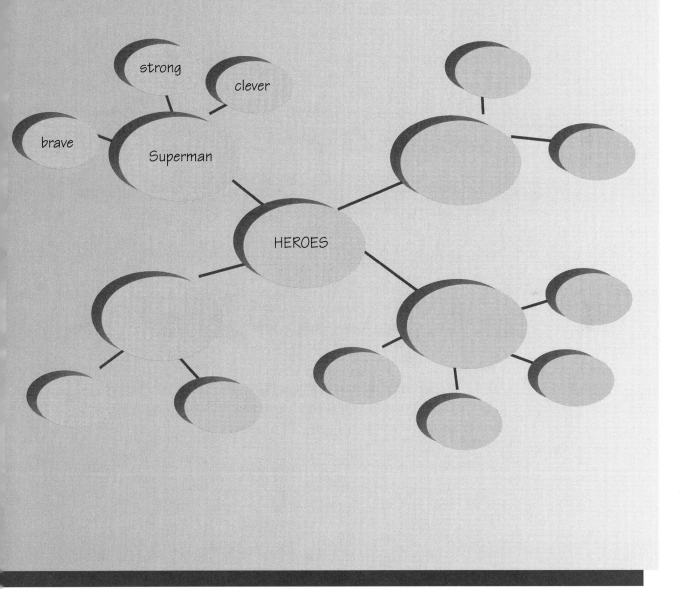

Have you heard of Roberto Clemente? Who was he? What do you already know about him? Discuss with your class.

Roberto Clemente was a hero. He was also one of the best baseball players of all time. He was both Latin American and black, and he was very proud of his roots. He grew up in the Barrio San Anton of Carolina, Puerto Rico. What made him a hero? Read this poem to find out.

roots Where he came from; his culture.

barrio The Spanish word for neighborhood.

guava tree A tree having white flowers and fruit that can be eaten.

fate In this case, the final result.

abound To have a great amount.

meekly Here it means without force or strength.

The Man From Puerto Rico: Roberto Clemente

Mark Daniels

A muddy field in San Anton.
Twelve boys of black and shades of brown.
Their baseball was of rags made round.

The bat was from the guava tree.
Their team was losing five to three.
Could Roberto bring them victory?

The Puerto Rican stepped to the plate.
A home run just might be his fate.
He hugged the bat. He couldn't wait.

Roberto swung at the rags made round.
With all his might and strength abound.
But the ball rolled meekly to the ground.

Later at home Roberto wailed,
"Papa, I know that I have failed."
But Papa's kindly wisdom soon prevailed.

"Roberto," his father took care to explain.
"There'll be other games to bring you fame.
You must work hard, my little Momen."

"You must be honest. You must meet your own needs.
But remain worthy. You'll be judged by your deeds.
We are a proud people. We plant our own seeds."

"Remember where you come from. You are a Jibaro.
Look to our past to prepare for tomorrow.
This is the way of dignity, the way of a hero."

The words of his father he never forgot.
With hard work he did well just as he was taught.
He joined the major leagues, a goal he had sought.

What made him a hero as the story is recounted,
Was not titles, nor honors, nor medals he mounted.
But warmth and compassion and service undaunted.

Nicaragua was shaken in nineteen seventy-two.
An earthquake killed thousands and supplies couldn't get through.
Roberto wanted to help. "It's the least I can do."

"Babies are dying. They all need supplies."
A cargo plane was loaded, and made ready to fly.
Roberto kissed his wife and his children good-bye.

wailed Cried loudly.

prevailed Won or had greater strength.

Momen A made-up name given to Roberto by his sister Rosa.

worthy Honorable.

deeds The things a person does.

Jibaro (pronounced hee-báh-roh) One who belongs to a special group of Puerto Ricans.

dignity Having self-respect.

major leagues The highest level of baseball teams.

recounted Retold.

titles Names given to honor people.

medals Pieces made out of metal (often shaped like coins) to honor people.

mounted Increased the number of.

compassion A caring for others who are suffering.

undaunted Here it means dependable and steady.

shaken Moved back and forth by a strong force.

cargo plane A plane that carries supplies.

The plane, old and heavily-loaded, struggled to fly.
It banked left, hit the ocean, never reaching the sky.
With so much to live for, he didn't want to die.

After his death, Roberto was proclaimed
To be the first Latin American to have gained
Election to the Baseball Hall of Fame.

The words of his father had come to fruition.
Give to others in need had become his son's mission.
His art was a blending of talent and compassion.

heavily-loaded
Carrying a great
quantity.

struggled Made a great
effort.

banked left Turned to
the left.

proclaimed Said or
announced in public.

election Selecting by
taking a vote.

Baseball Hall of Fame
A place where baseball
players are honored.

fruition Made
something good
happen.

blending A coming
together.

WITH YOUR CLASS ▼

Think about the poem. Discuss it with your class and the teacher. The questions below may help you.

1. Tell about Roberto's early experience with baseball. Where did he play? What was it like there? With whom did he play? What does this experience tell you about his early childhood?

2. Roberto told his father, "I know that I have failed." Why did he think he had failed?

3. What advice did Roberto's father give him? Do you think the father's advice was good?

4. What do you think the father meant when he said, "We are a proud people. We plant our own seeds"?

5. What do you think the father meant when he said, "Look to the past to prepare for tomorrow"? How can the past help people get ready for what is to come?

6. What happened in Nicaragua? What did Roberto do to help?

7. How did Roberto die? Why was his death so tragic or sad?

8. What great honor did Roberto Clemente receive?

9. According to the poem, what made Roberto a hero? What qualities did he have?

WITH A SMALL GROUP

Roberto's father said that his people are a proud people. Think about the traditions or ways of doing things in the culture you know best. Which ones make you most proud? Share them with a small group. Include the qualities of the people, their daily activities, songs, art, etc. You may want to bring some things from home to talk about with your small group.

Looking at Literature

NARRATIVE POETRY

You learned in Unit 1 (page 19) that lyric poems describe feelings or ideas. Narrative poems, on the other hand, tell a story. Is the poem about Roberto Clemente a narrative poem or a lyric poem? Discuss with your class and the teacher.

USING RHYME AND NEAR-RHYME

Words rhyme when their endings sound exactly the same. For example, the words "way" and "say" rhyme. If their endings are only similar and not exactly the same, we call this *near-rhyme*. An example of near-rhyme are the words "way" and "bye."

Below are words that end some of the lines from the poem about Roberto Clemente. With your class and the teacher discuss whether they are rhyme or near-rhyme.

plate	Anton	wailed	needs
fate	brown	failed	deeds
wait	round	prevailed	seeds

Now look back at the other poems you have read so far in this book. Do any of them use rhyme or near-rhyme? Note that the rhyming lines do not have to come one right after the other. But they do have to be close.

With a partner, see if you can make up two lines that rhyme to describe Roberto Clemente. You may want to share them with your class.

Have you ever known about any animals in danger? If so, tell a partner about them. Was there anything you could do to help?

Pablo Red Deer, a Papago Indian, has just finished the school year. He is hired to be a flagman on a road crew for the summer. He soon discovers that the men in the crew are making plans to trap the coyotes in the area. The government wants to limit the number of coyotes and is paying people to trap and kill them. Now to Pablo, coyotes are not animals to be killed. They are creatures of great strength, beauty, and wisdom. He must do something to stop their destruction. Is he a hero? Read about Pablo's first night with the road crew.

from

He-Who-Runs-Far

Hazel Fredericksen

AFTER SUPPER that night some of the men sat around the campfire talking. Pablo, sitting a little apart, suddenly heard the word "coyote." He moved closer, not wishing to miss anything they were saying.

"There are coyotes around here all right," one man said. "Last time we were here I heard them almost every night. We didn't have any traps though."

"Bill brought traps this time," a second man said.

"We can get two-fifty bounty for each pair of ears."

"How many traps did you bring, Bill?"

"Couple a' dozen. They're all in a gunnysack in the pickup. Better wait to set them until the moon comes up so we can see."

A great resolve was forming in Pablo's mind. He must find those traps. He must destroy them before these men could set them. He must save the coyotes. The pickup truck stood in the shadow of one of the big bulldozers. Pablo got up casually and walked toward it. When he was about to climb into the back, someone called, "Hey, kid, where you going?" Pablo jumped and mumbled something about getting his jacket. Then he turned and walked to the tent where he was supposed to sleep.

After waiting a while, he looked out at the truck. Maybe the way would be clear now. The men were still laughing and talking around the fire, but the moon would soon be up. He must move quickly.

He crept out of the tent making no sound. There were twenty feet to the truck. Anyone looking could see. Pablo had to take that chance. Seven silent steps. He made it. Now he was pulling himself into the pickup. The gunnysack was there. He grasped the sack and moved it a little. It was very heavy. It was the traps all right. He knew he could carry them. But he had to get the sack out where he could lift it on his back. He took off his jacket and laid it over the pickup's tailgate to deaden any noise.

Just then one of the men came stumbling up the path. He went right past the tailgate of the truck. Pablo curled up like another gunnysack. The man went by without noticing—but would he see Pablo on the way back? The wait seemed endless. Then Pablo heard him coming again. An empty bottle clattered on the floor of the pickup beside Pablo. A hand grasped the tailgate covered by Pablo's jacket. For a minute the man teetered, then steadying himself, he stumbled back to the fire.

Pablo got to work again. He got the sack onto the jacket and slipped his body past it onto the ground. He listened carefully. So far all seemed safe. He bent over and managed to get the sack on his back and ease himself up. Slowly he moved to a group of low trees on the far side of the camp. He paused to adjust the weight of the sack on his back. Then he started moving toward the edge of a canyon he had seen as they rode into camp the day before.

He had to destroy these traps, but how? Breaking them with rocks would make too much noise. What else could he do? As he crept to where he could look over a ledge, he got his answer. First he heard a faint swirling, gurgling sound; then far below he made out a rushing of water over steep rocks. If he could get the traps down into this waterfall, they might never be found. And if they were found, they would be too rusty to use.

He lugged the sack to a high place almost directly over the falls. A mighty push sent it out into clear space and crashing and splashing into the falls below.

He crawled back over the ledge to the flat land above. The pale moon was beginning to show. Soon the men would be hunting for their traps. He thought, "I'd better circle back, get into bed, and pretend to be asleep when they start looking."

stumbling Almost falling down.

clattered Made loud noises as it hit the hard surface and bounced.

teetered Stood but moved back and forth, almost falling.

steadying Controlling his movement.

adjust Change slightly for better balance.

canyon A long narrow valley with sides that rise sharply.

swirling Going around in a circle.

gurgling Sounding like water running unevenly, perhaps over rocks.

made out Could barely hear.

steep Rising sharply.

rusty Turned orange and rough by the water.

lugged Pulled or carried with much difficulty.

At a clump of trees he stopped. There was a murmur of men's voices. He ran to the nearest tree, grabbed a lower branch and pulled himself up among the thick, low-hanging limbs. The voices were angry. "He's hiding somewhere around here."

"Hey! I've some hound dogs back home. They'd take one sniff of this jacket he left and track him."

A second voice answered, "He couldn't have gone far. Those traps are too heavy. It'll take him hours to lug them into town to sell or trade them. Might as well wait until daylight."

Pablo waited until he could no longer hear the sounds of feet. Then he climbed slowly down and sat crouched on the ground at the foot of the tree. Where should he go? Not back to camp, that was for sure.

He rubbed his hands together. The late spring nights were cold, and he missed his jacket. He knew he must get moving.

All night Pablo went west, half walking, half running, guided by the stars. He felt safe. He knew that there must be twenty miles between him and the camp now. When the sun rose he stopped for a while to rest by a small, rippling creek. He found a clump of heavy brush, crawled in and slept.

When he awakened, the heat of the day had passed. Night was coming on again. He bathed his face and hands, drank deeply of water, and started on. Now he traveled away from the foothills toward the valley. He walked fast in the twilight, thinking about food. Then he stopped suddenly. Did he smell coffee on the little breeze that was blowing? No, of

clump Group.

murmur A low sound of voices, but the words are run together and cannot be heard.

sniff Smell.

track Here it means to find him by knowing his smell.

crouched Bent over.

rippling Moving in little waves.

brush Here it means small bushes.

foothills Small hills at the foot, or base, of a mountain.

course not. Thinking about food was making him imagine things. Then he was hit by a fear that somehow he had walked in a circle back toward the road crew's camp. His sense of direction told him this was not so, and the stars confirmed that feeling. Yet, he was now really sure he smelled coffee. His first impulse was to turn back into the hills but hunger and curiosity urged him on. He came to a clearing. There in front of him was a man squatting over a small fire, stirring something in a pan. On the coals a coffee pot bubbled. Pablo saw the man rise to his feet. Pablo drew back hurriedly. The man's hand flew to a gun holster on his hip.

"Who's there?" His voice was level and without panic.

Pablo hesitated, then stepped forward into the firelight. "You alone?" the man asked. His eyes were steady and his hand was still on the gun.

"Yes, sir." Pablo suddenly was not afraid of this stranger. This man would only hurt another if he must protect himself.

"What are you doing way out here on foot?" The man peered at him more closely.

"I got lost," Pablo said briefly. The man looked at him with a skeptical smile. He held out his hand.

"My name's Walker," he said. "Bob Walker." Pablo shook hands lightly.

"I am Pablo." Then he added softly, "Red Deer. . . ."

"Hungry?" the man asked, noticing that Pablo had not been able to keep his eyes away from the cooking pan over the fire.

"Yes, sir. Very hungry."

confirmed Supported.

impulse A sudden desire to act in a certain way

curiosity A strong desire to learn about something.

urged Pushed or strongly encouraged.

squatting Sitting on one's heels.

bubbled Formed bubbles on top.

holster A case for a gun which is worn on the body.

panic Extreme fear.

hesitated Waited briefly.

peered Looked.

skeptical Disbelieving.

stew A thick soup made of cooked meat and vegetables.

The man laughed and walked to the fire. "Plenty of stew here, such as it is." He filled a tin plate and handed it to Pablo. "Help yourself to coffee." He pointed to a tin cup nearby. They ate silently. The man asked no questions. When they finished, they sat watching the dying fire.

WITH YOUR CLASS ▼

Think about the story. Discuss it with your class and the teacher. The questions below may help you.

1. Why are the men planning to trap the coyotes in the area? What will they do with them?

2. Why do you think the plan to trap the coyotes was so upsetting to Pablo? What does he resolve to do about it?

3. Why does he have to act before the moon comes up?

4. A man stumbles to the pickup truck when Pablo is trying to get to the traps. Why is the man stumbling? What do you think is wrong with him?

5. What did Pablo do to the traps? Will the men be able to use them again? Explain. Do you think it was right for Pablo to take the traps? Why or why not?

6. Why did Pablo decide to leave the men? Tell about how he got away.

7. What error does Pablo think he has made when he first smells coffee? Where is the smell coming from?

8. Was Pablo afraid of the man with the gun? Why or why not?

9. Do you think the man and the boy like each other? How do you know?

10. Is Pablo a hero? If so, in what ways? Are there people in the story who would not call him a hero? Explain.

WITH A SMALL GROUP ▼

Think about the questions below. Discuss one or both with a small group.

1. Have you or someone you know had an experience similar to Pablo's? If so, tell what happened.

2. Some people feel that the coyote is a destructive animal that should be destroyed. It sometimes kills farm animals and pets for food. Do you think there could be other ways to deal with a problem such as this?

Write a letter to Pablo. Tell him how you feel about his actions to save the coyotes. See the letter form on page 17. Give your letter to a partner. Ask your partner to pretend to be Pablo and answer your letter.

The Conflict in a Story

Most stories have a conflict or a sort of war between the characters. Usually there is a protagonist (pronounced pro-tág-o-nist). The protagonist is often the main character. Working against the protagonist is the antagonist (pronounced an-tág-o-nist). The antagonist does not want the protagonist to win.

Now think about the story "He–Who–Runs–Far." Discuss the conflict with your class and the teacher. Answer the questions below.

> Who is the protagonist?
> What does the protagonist want?
> Who is the antagonist?
> What does the antagonist want?

It is important to know that the protagonist and the antagonist can also be groups of characters instead of just one character or thing.

The Plot or Chain of Events

Make a chain of events for the plot of "He–Who–Runs–Far." Use the chain of events you made for "My Name Is San Ho" as an example (see page 43). Remember to include only those events that you think are important. Your first two links might look something like this:

Compare your chain of events with that of a partner. Make any changes you want based on what you learn.

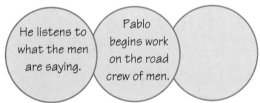

He listens to what the men are saying.

Pablo begins work on the road crew of men.

The Climax of a Story

The conflict between the protagonist and the antagonist usually builds to a high point called the climax. The climax is the most exciting part of the story. Will the protagonist win? Or will the antagonist win? Look again at the chain of events you just made for "He–Who–Runs– Far." Which link has the most exciting event in it? Write the word "CLIMAX" beside it. Then discuss it with your class and the teacher.

Many heroes put themselves in great danger to help others. But are there other kinds of heroes? Think about Calvin and what he does in the cartoon below.

Calvin and Hobbes

By Bill Watterson

Calvin and Hobbes

by Bill Watterson

WITH YOUR CLASS

Discuss the following questions about "Calvin and Hobbs" with your class and the teacher.

1. What does Calvin do in the cartoon? Do you think what he does is unusual? Why or why not? How does he feel about doing it? What is the result of this action?

2. Do you think the cartoon is funny? Explain.

3. Do you think that Calvin is a hero? Why or why not? Do the actions of a hero always have to be big and full of excitement? Can they also be just small acts—perhaps of kindness? Explain.

WITH A SMALL GROUP

Think of someone who, like Calvin, may have acted in kindness—no matter how small the act. Tell your group about that person. What was the situation? What did that person do?

Often it is not just one action or set of actions that makes a person a hero. It may be the way a person lives each day, especially if that person has trouble walking because of a physical disability. What do you think it might be like to not be able to walk or move like everyone else? What would it be like to go to school? Discuss with your class. Then read this autobiographical sketch by Melissa Medrano to find out how she was able to live with her disability.

challenge A test of courage or skill.

bunched up Here it means bent together at the knees.

abusing Here it means harming the body.

osteogenesis imperfecta (pronounced aw-stee-o-gén-uh-sis im-per-féc-tuh).

genetic Passed from the parents to their children through cells called genes. The genes control such things as hair color, etc.

calcium A metal that is found in bones and teeth. It is needed for normal strength. The next sentence is a clue.

brittle Hard but easy to break.

shock A serious upset to the mind and body caused by a sudden, very unpleasant event.

from

MY CHALLENGE

Melissa Medrano, Age 13

I WAS BORN with both of my legs broken. When my parents took me home from the hospital, they noticed that I always kept my legs bunched up. In the beginning they didn't realize anything was wrong, but when I started screaming every time they changed my diaper, they got worried. They took me to the doctor right away.

At first, the doctors thought my parents were abusing me. Then they did some tests and found out that I have a rare bone disease called osteogenesis imperfecta. It's a genetic disease. It means that my bones don't use calcium the way other people's bones do. This makes them very brittle and soft, so they break easily. One time my leg broke, just because I was sitting down the wrong way.

Breaking a bone is awful. It feels like a whole bunch of knives going into you. The funny thing is, at first you don't really feel the pain because you're in shock—you feel like you're flying through the air. It is very scary.

Swimming is the best exercise for me because even if I fall, I can't really hurt myself. It also helps me to build strength. In the summer when I'm more active, I notice that I'm a lot stronger. My doctor tells me the more exercise I get, the less trouble my bones will have absorbing calcium.

I had my first operation when I was seven. The big bone that goes from my hip to my knee had broken in several places. They took it out and put a metal rod inside it. I've had nine surgeries since, all to put rods in my legs. The rods act as braces—they help me stand up and they prevent my bones from breaking so easily. Whenever one of my legs outgrows a rod, the doctors have to make an incision in my leg and put in a longer rod.

Sometimes I have to stay in the hospital several months for rehabilitation. It's not easy to be away from home, especially because I don't get to see my family much. My parents both work and so I usually only get to see them when they take me home on weekends.

I work with my physical therapist two or three times a day and we do exercises like side leg lifts, sit-ups, and riding an exercise bike. She is really cool and fun to be with, and if I ever have a problem I know I can go and talk to her about it. She is one of the people who makes staying at the hospital a little easier. Also I'm pretty close to some of the nurses, since they're around a lot more than the doctors. Being around there so much has made me want to be a pediatrician when I grow up. I'd like to work with children, and I think it would be very rewarding to be a surgeon or to work in a clinic.

Besides missing school, one of the worst things about being in the hospital all the time is having no privacy. Some doctors are just rude. Sometimes, they walk into my room without knocking when I'm dressing. I tell them nicely to get out. They usually get embarrassed and apologize. One time a doctor brought a whole group of residents into my

absorbing Here it means taking in.

operation (another word for "surgery") Cutting into the body to repair it.

incision A cut made with a knife.

rehabilitation A program to help a person become as active and healthy as before.

physical therapist A person who has had special training to help people use parts of their body again.

sit-ups Exercises done by lying flat on one's back on the floor and sitting up over and over again.

exercise bike A bike that does not go anywhere when a person rides it.

cool Nice.

pediatrician A children's doctor.

surgeon A doctor who operates or does surgery.

privacy Time to be alone with no one watching or listening.

apologize To say you are sorry.

Melissa Medrano uses a long pole with a clamp attached to the end to pick up her slipper.

room without any warning. I talked to him about it, and now he gives me lots of notice if he's bringing people to see me.

The other time when I don't get along with the residents that well is when I'm in pain. For example, when something hurts, I usually try not to show it. The problem is, when I do say I feel pain and I need medication, some of the residents think I'm kidding. They expect me to be lying down and crying when it hurts. I don't like anyone to see me that way.

I now have a sister, Christina. She is ten years old and she has osteogenesis imperfecta, too, but not as bad as I do. I think she has a harder time dealing with it. Sometimes when she breaks a leg, she says she wishes she weren't alive. I tell her she'll get over it, that she won't always feel that way. I think that getting through all my operations has given me a lot of courage. I'm trying to pass it along to her.

Even though my disease is getting better with time, I'm not very independent. My knees and waist are weak. I need to use a long pole with a clamp attached to the end to pick things up from the floor. The disease has also affected my hearing. The bones in my ear are much softer and weaker than other people's and they break a lot more easily. The doctors have told me that by the time I'm thirty, there's a chance I'll be half deaf. But I don't always believe everything the doctors tell me.

In the fall, I'm starting high school. It makes me feel good to know that I've come as far as I have with my disease. I'm excited, because I feel like it will be the beginning of a whole new life.

residents Here it means doctors who are receiving special training.

notice Here it means warning that something is going to happen.

medication Medicine.

kidding Teasing or not serious.

dealing with Taking action about.

independent Able to live without help from others.

clamp Here it means a tool that is used to grab objects (see the picture on page 104).

attached Connected to.

affected Caused something to change.

WITH YOUR CLASS ▼

Think about the story. Discuss it with your class and the teacher. The questions below may help you.

1. How did Melissa's parents know that something was wrong with her when she was a baby?

2. What did the doctors think was wrong with Melissa at first? What might have caused them to think that?

3. Describe her disease. Why did she have to have so many surgeries?

4. What was the best exercise for Melissa? Why? Why did the doctor think that exercise was very important for her?

5. What people made her hospital stay easier? Explain.

6. What advice did she give her sister who also has the same disease? Do you agree with her advice? What would you have said?

7. How does she feel about going to high school? Why do you think she feels this way?

8. Do you think Melissa is a hero? If so, what qualities does she have that make her one?

WITH A PARTNER ▼

Discuss one or both questions with a partner.

1. Do you know of a person who has a disability? Who is that person? What problems does that person have? In what ways are that person's problems similar to those of Melissa? What qualities does that person have that you admire? In your opinion, is that person a hero? Why or why not? Share your thoughts with a partner.

2. Melissa says that her physical therapist is someone she can talk to about problems. Do you have someone in your life that you can talk to about problems? Who is that person? Why do you feel comfortable with that person?

WITH A SMALL GROUP

Think about the questions below. Then discuss at least two of them with a small group.

1. Melissa tells about times when doctors and residents came into her room without telling her they were coming. How do you think it would feel to not have any privacy? What would you have said to the doctors?

2. Melissa says that ". . . when something hurts, I usually try not to show it." What happened to her in the hospital when she tried to hide her pain? Is it a good idea to not show pain when you feel it? Why or why not?

3. Being around doctors a lot made Melissa want to be one. Have you ever wanted to do the same kind of work as a person or people you were around a lot? Explain.

WITH YOUR CLASS ▼

Discuss the following questions with your class and the teacher.

1. Can a person who has overcome great problems, not just physical ones, be a hero? Think, for example, of people who have overcome poverty, a painful divorce, or a death in the family. In what ways might these people also be thought of as heroes?

2. Does a hero always have to act like a hero? Is it possible for the same person to be a hero in some cases but not in others? Discuss with your class and the teacher.

Write about the time when you may have acted like a hero. Describe the events that happened and explain why you think your actions may have been heroic. Remember to place the date by your entry and state your topic (see the example on page 16). If you want to, you can share what you write with a partner. Think of your own questions to ask.

Now that you have read this unit, think about the people you admire most. They may be famous people, such as sports figures like Roberto Clemente. They may be friends who want to do something kind, like Pablo Red Deer or Calvin in the cartoon. Or, they may be people who have lived with great difficulties, such as Melissa Medrano. Write the names of these people you admire and decide what it is that you admire most about them. On your paper make a chart similar to the one below.

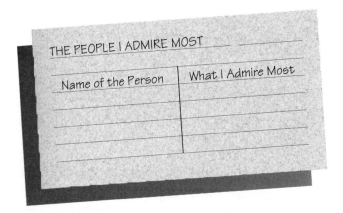

THE PEOPLE I ADMIRE MOST

Name of the Person	What I Admire Most

Share your chart with a small group. Discuss why you admire each person you have listed. Then add their names to the chart your class made of heroes at the beginning of this unit unless their names are already there. Make sure you write on the chart why each is a hero.

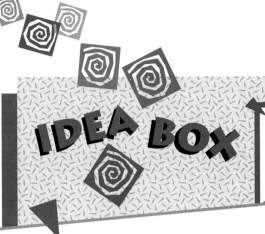

IDEA BOX

DEVELOPING YOUR WORD BANK

Continue developing your Work Bank. See the directions on page 24.

Choral Reading

Choral reading is reading out loud together. With your class, read together the poem about Roberto Clemente. Your teacher may want to divide you into groups to read different sections or stanzas of the poem. Individuals might volunteer to read solo parts.

Practice the choral reading several times and present it to another class or invite one or more guests to come in and hear your performance. Your teacher may want to record it on an audio or videotape for future listening.

Your Own Autobiographical Sketch

Write your own autobiographical sketch. You may use Melissa Medrano's sketch as an example. Include details about your life such as where you live, details about school, your family and friends, the problems you have overcome, and your future plans. You can share your sketch with a partner and later with your teacher.

A Famous Hero as a Friend

If you could choose one famous hero of the past or of the present to be your friend, whom would you choose? Once you decide, go to the library and find out as much as you can about that person. Come back and share the information with a small group. Tell your group why you would like that person to be your friend.

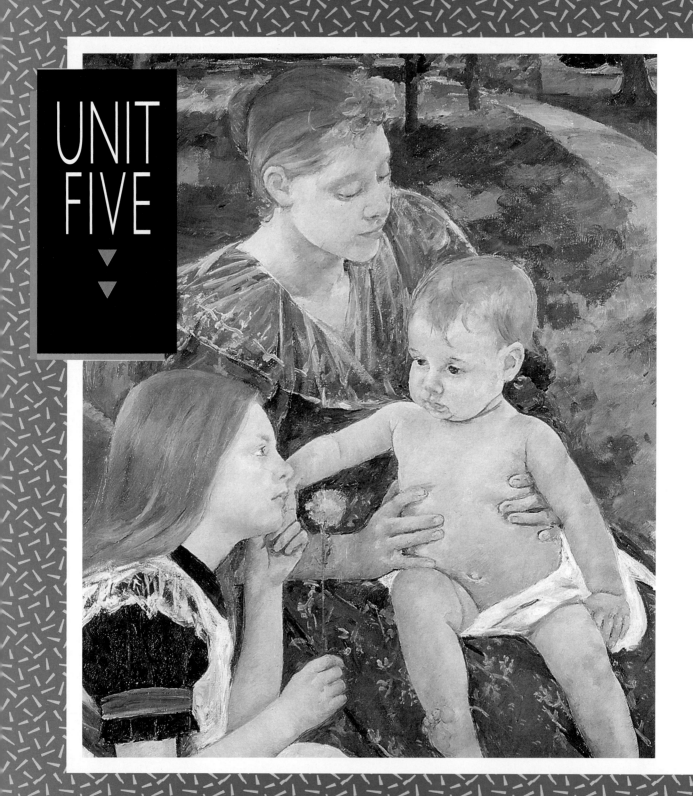

Faces of Love

Love is what holds our friendships, families, and our own worlds together. In this unit you will read about love's different "faces." Just as people have different faces, so does love. There are many kinds of love that people can experience. Learn how important these different kinds of love can be to us and to those with whom we live.

▼

Getting Started

Think about all the different kinds of love that you have experienced. Although romantic love is the kind of love we most often hear about, it is not the only kind of love. And it is not always the best kind of love. Using a cloud diagram like the one below, name as many different kinds of love as you can think of. Use the picture that begins this unit to help you think of different kinds of love.

Kinds of Love

Love of animals or pets

What is Love?

Here are some common dictionary definitions:

1. a strong affection for or attachment to a person or persons
2. a strong liking for or interest in something
3. a strong, usually passionate affection for another person

With a partner, look again at your cloud diagram. On your paper make a chart similar to the one below. Choose a few kinds of love to include on your chart. Under each kind of love, write down different ways in which that love can be expressed or shown to others.

DIFFERENT KINDS OF LOVE
AND HOW EACH CAN BE EXPRESSED

Love of animals or pets		
—taking my dog for a walk every day		

When you and your partner have completed your charts, join another pair of classmates. Share your charts and discuss the kinds of love and how each can be shown or expressed. You may want to add items to your chart based on what you learn.

The following picture-poetry helps us see what the word "love" can mean to a person. Read to find out where the author has discovered different faces of love.

from

Love Is a Special Way of Feeling

Joan Walsh Anglund

Love is found in unexpected places . . .
It is there in the quiet moment
when we first discover a beautiful thing . . .
when we watch a bird soar against a pale blue sky . . .

soar To fly swiftly upward.

when we see a lovely flower that no one else has noticed . . .

Love starts in little ways . . .
It may begin the day we first share our
thoughts with someone else . . .

Or, sometimes, it begins because,
even without words,
we understand how someone feels.

WITH YOUR CLASS

Discuss the picture-poetry with your class and the teacher. You may want to use the questions below to help you.

1. What does the poet find to love in the world around her? What different kinds of love does she experience?

2. Describe the love between friends talked about on page 116. Why do you think the poet says, "Love starts in little ways . . ."?

Try one or both of the following activities.

1. Describe in writing a spot somewhere outdoors that you especially love. Tell why this place is so special to you. What do you see when you are there? What do you hear? How does it make you feel to be there? You may want to include a drawing or a photograph of this place with your description. Share you work with a partner.

2. The poet talks about love and where it begins. She says that it begins when we are able to share our thoughts with someone else. Write about a friend you can share your inner thoughts with. Tell why it is possible for you to share personal things with this friend. Describe the feelings you have when you spend time with this special person. Share your writing with a partner.

The following story is from the novel Sarah, Plain and Tall. *It tells of several kinds of love—love that is new and fragile and love that is so strong and powerful that it can even survive death. Read about a family's love for one another and how that love is deepened by a stranger who comes into their lives.*

from

Sarah, Plain and Tall

Patricia MacLachlan

fragile Easily broken.

survive Stay alive; live longer.

every–single–day An expression meaning each day.

dusk The beginning of darkness in the evening.

hearthstones The stones surrounding a fireplace.

hollow Sounding like a noise made in a place that is empty.

stirred Moved.

slab A thick slice.

bread dough A mixture of flour and liquid for making bread.

crackled Made snapping sounds.

"DID MAMA sing every day?" asked Caleb. "Every–single–day?" He sat close to the fire, his chin in his hand. It was dusk, and the dogs lay beside him on the warm hearthstones.

"Every–single–day," I told him for the second time this week. For the twentieth time this month. The hundredth time this year? And the past few years?

"And did Papa sing, too?"

"Yes. Papa sang, too. Don't get so close, Caleb. You'll heat up."

He pushed his chair back. It made a hollow scraping sound on the hearthstones, and the dogs stirred. Lottie, small and black, wagged her tail and lifted her head. Nick slept on.

I turned the bread dough over and over on the marble slab on the kitchen table.

"Well, Papa doesn't sing anymore," said Caleb very softly. A log broke apart and crackled in the fireplace. He looked up at me. "What did I look like when I was born?"

"You didn't have any clothes on," I told him.

"I know that," he said.

Christopher Walken as Papa, Glenn Close as Sarah, Christopher
Bell as Caleb, and Lexi Randall as Anna in the television movie
"Sarah, Plain and Tall."

"You looked like this." I held the bread dough up in a round pale ball.

"I had hair," said Caleb seriously.

"And she named me Caleb," he went on, filling in the old familiar story.

"I would have named you Troublesome," I said, making Caleb smile.

"And Mama handed me to you in the yellow blanket and said . . ." He waited for me to finish the story. "And said . . . ?"

I sighed. "And Mama said, 'Isn't he beautiful, Anna?'"

"And I was," Caleb finished.

Caleb thought the story was over, and I didn't tell him what I had really thought. He was homely and plain, and he had a terrible holler and a horrid smell. But these were not the worst of him. Mama died the next morning. That was the worst thing about Caleb.

"Isn't he beautiful, Anna?" Her last words to me. I had gone to bed thinking how wretched he looked. And I forgot to say good night.

I wiped my hands on my apron and went to the window. Outside, the prairie reached out and touched the places where the sky came down. Though winter was nearly over, there were patches of snow and ice everywhere. I looked at the long dirt road that crawled across the plains, remembering the morning that Mama had died, cruel and sunny. They had come for her in a wagon and taken her away to be buried. And then the cousins and aunts and uncles had come and tried to fill up the house. But they couldn't.

Slowly, one by one, they left. And then the days seemed long and dark like winter days, even though it wasn't winter. And Papa didn't sing.

Isn't he beautiful, Anna?

No, Mama.

pale Light colored.

troublesome Causing trouble.

homely Ugly; not attractive.

holler A loud cry.

wretched Miserable; very unhappy.

prairie A large area of flat, rolling grassland.

It was hard to think of Caleb as beautiful. It took three whole days for me to love him, sitting in the chair by the fire, Papa washing up the supper dishes, Caleb's tiny hand brushing my cheek. And a smile. It was the smile, I know.

"Can you remember her songs?" asked Caleb. "Mama's songs?"

I turned from the window. "No. Only that she sang about flowers and birds. Sometimes about the moon at nighttime."

Caleb reached down and touched Lottie's head.

"Maybe," he said, his voice low, "if you remember the songs, then I might remember her, too."

My eyes widened and tears came. Then the door opened and wind blew in with Papa, and I went to stir the stew. Papa put his arms around me and put his nose in my hair.

"Nice soapy smell, that stew," he said.

I laughed. "That's my hair."

Caleb came over and threw his arms around Papa's neck and hung down as Papa swung him back and forth, and the dogs sat up.

"Cold in town," said Papa. "And Jack was feisty." Jack was Papa's horse that he'd raised from a colt. "Rascal," murmured Papa, smiling, because no matter what Jack did Papa loved him.

I spooned up the stew and lighted the oil lamp and we ate with the dogs crowding under the table, hoping for spills and handouts.

Papa might not have told us about Sarah that night if Caleb hadn't asked him the question. After the dishes were cleared and washed and Papa was filling the tin pail with ashes, Caleb spoke up. It wasn't a question, really.

"You don't sing anymore," he said. He said it harshly. Not because he meant to, but because he had been thinking of it for so long. "Why?" he asked more gently.

feisty Lively, very active.

colt A young horse, not fully grown.

rascal A worthless person (often used jokingly).

handouts Food or gifts given freely.

Slowly Papa straightened up. There was a long silence, and the dogs looked up, wondering at it.

"I've forgotten the old songs," said Papa quietly. He sat down. "But maybe there's a way to remember them." He looked up at us.

"How?" asked Caleb eagerly.

Papa leaned back in the chair. "I've placed an advertisement in the newspapers. For help."

"You mean a housekeeper?" I asked, surprised.

Caleb and I looked at each other and burst out laughing, remembering Hilly, our old housekeeper. She was round and slow and shuffling. She snored in a high whistle at night, like a teakettle, and let the fire go out.

"No," said Papa slowly. "Not a housekeeper." He paused. "A wife."

Caleb started at Papa. "A wife? You mean a mother?"

Nick slid his face onto Papa's lap and Papa stroked his ears.

"That, too," said Papa. "Like Maggie."

Matthew, our neighbor to the south, had written to ask for a wife and mother for his children. And Maggie had come from Tennessee. Her hair was the color of turnips and she laughed.

Papa reached into his pocket and unfolded a letter written on white paper.

"And I have received an answer." Papa read to us:

> Dear Mr. Jacob Witting,
> I am Sarah Wheaton from Maine as you will see from my letter. I am answering your advertisement. I have never been married, though I have been asked. I have lived with an older brother, William, who is about to be married. His wife-to-be is young and energetic.
> I have always loved to live by the sea, but at this time I feel a move is necessary. And the truth is, the sea is as

eagerly With a very strong interest.

advertisement A paid public announcement.

housekeeper Someone hired to take care of the housework.

shuffling With a sliding walk.

teakettle A covered pot with a spout. Used for boiling water to make tea.

stroked Gently rubbed.

turnips A round lightly colored root eaten as a vegetable.

wife-to-be The wife that he will soon have.

energetic Strong and very active.

far east as I can go. My choice, as you can see, is limited. This should not be taken as an insult. I am strong and I work hard and I am willing to travel. But I am not mild mannered. If you should still care to write, I would be interested in your children and about where you live. And you.

Very truly yours,
Sarah Elisabeth Wheaton
P.S. Do you have opinions on cats? I have one.

No one spoke when Papa finished the letter. He kept looking at it in his hands, reading it over to himself. Finally I turned my head a bit to sneak a look at Caleb. He was smiling. I smiled, too.

"One thing," I said in the quiet of the room.

"What's that?" asked Papa, looking up.

I put my arm around Caleb.

"Ask her if she sings," I said.

2

The dogs loved Sarah first. Lottie slept beside her bed, curled in a soft circle, and Nick leaned his face on the covers in the morning, watching for the first sign that Sarah was awake. No one knew where Seal, Sarah's cat, slept. Seal was a roamer.

Sarah's collection of shells sat on the windowsill.

"A scallop," she told us, picking up the shells one by one, "a sea clam, an oyster, a razor clam. And a conch shell. If you put it to your ear you can hear the sea." She put it to Caleb's ear, then mine. Papa listened, too. Then Sarah listened once more, with a look so sad and far away that Caleb leaned against me.

limited Restricted; only having a few.

insult A comment intended to hurt someone's feelings.

mild mannered Gentle in the way one acts.

opinions What one thinks; judgments.

roamer Someone who moves from one place to another a lot. The sentence before is a clue.

scallop, sea clam, oyster, razor clam Sea animals having hard outer shells.

conch shell A large, spiral shell.

Christopher Bell as Caleb and Glenn Close as Sarah, in the television movie "Sarah, Plain and Tall."

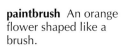

"At least Sarah can hear the sea," he whispered.

Papa was shy and quiet with Sarah, and so was I. But Caleb talked to Sarah from morning until the light left the sky.

"Where are you going?" he asked. "To do what?"

"To pick flowers," said Sarah. "I'll hang some of them upside down and dry them so they'll keep some color. And we can have flowers all winter long."

"I'll come, too!" cried Caleb. "Sarah said winter," he said to me. "That means Sarah will stay."

Together we picked flowers, paintbrush and clover and prairie violets. There were buds on the wild roses that climbed up the paddock fence.

"The roses will bloom in early summer," I told Sarah. I looked to see if she knew what I was thinking. Summer was when the wedding would be. Might be. Sarah and Papa's wedding.

We hung the flowers from the ceiling in little bunches. "I've never seen this before," said Sarah. "What is it called?"

"Bride's bonnet," I told her.

Caleb smiled at the name.

"We don't have this by the sea," she said. "We have seaside goldenrod and wild asters and woolly ragwort."

"Woolly ragwort!" Caleb whooped. He made up a song.

> *"Woolly ragwort all around,*
> *Woolly ragwort on the ground.*
> *Woolly ragwort grows and grows,*
> *Woolly ragwort in your nose."*

Sarah and Papa laughed, and the dogs lifted their heads and thumped their tails against the wood floor. Seal sat on a kitchen chair and watched us with yellow eyes.

We ate Sarah's stew, the late light coming through the windows. Papa had baked bread that was still warm from the fire.

paintbrush An orange flower shaped like a brush.

clover Low-growing plants with three leaves.

prairie violet A small purple flower growing on the prairie.

paddock A small enclosed field, often used for exercising animals.

bride's bonnet A flower in the shape of a bride's hat.

goldenrod Wild plants with yellow flowers.

wild asters Wild plants with spear-shaped leaves.

woolly ragwort A tall plant with yellow flowers.

"The stew is fine," said Papa.

"Ayuh." Sarah nodded. "The bread, too."

"What does 'ayuh' mean?" asked Caleb.

"In Maine it means yes," said Sarah. "Do you want more stew?"

"Ayuh," said Caleb.

"Ayuh," echoed my father.

After dinner Sarah told us about William. "He has a gray-and-white boat named Kittiwake." She looked out the window. "That is a small gull found way off the shore where William fishes. There are three aunts who live near us. They wear silk dresses and no shoes. You would love them."

"Ayuh," said Caleb.

"Does your brother look like you?" I asked.

"Yes," said Sarah. "He is plain and tall."

At dusk Sarah cut Caleb's hair on the front steps, gathering his curls and scattering them on the fence and ground. Seal batted some hair around the porch as the dogs watched.

"Why?" asked Caleb.

"For the birds," said Sarah. "They will use it for their nests. Later we can look for nests of curls."

"Sarah said 'later,'" Caleb whispered to me as we spread his hair about. "Sarah will stay."

Sarah cut Papa's hair, too. No one else saw, but I found him behind the barn, tossing the pieces of hair into the wind for the birds.

Sarah brushed my hair and tied it up in back with a rose velvet ribbon she had brought from Maine. She brushed hers long and free and tied it back, too, and we stood side by side looking into the mirror. I looked taller, like Sarah, and fair and thin. And with my hair pulled back I looked a little like her daughter. Sarah's daughter.

And then it was time for singing.

Sarah sang us a song we had never heard before as we sat

on the porch, insects buzzing in the dark, the rustle of cows in the grasses. It was called "Sumer Is Icumen in," and she taught it us all, even Papa, who sang as if he had never stopped singing.

"Sumer is icumen in,
Lhude sing cuccu!"

"What is sumer?" asked Caleb. He said it "soomer," the way Sarah had said it.

"Summer," said Papa and Sarah at the same time. Caleb and I looked at each other. Summer was coming.

"Tomorrow," said Sarah, "I want to see the sheep. You know, I've never touched one."

"Never?" Caleb sat up.

"Never," said Sarah. She smiled and leaned back in her chair. But I've touched seals. Real seals. They are cool and slippery and they slide through the water like fish. They can cry and sing. And sometimes they bark, a little like dogs."

Sarah barked like a seal. And Lottie and Nick came running from the barn to jump up on Sarah and lick her face and make her laugh. Sarah stroked them and scratched their ears and it was quiet again.

"I wish I could touch a seal right now," said Caleb, his voice soft in the night.

"So do I," said Sarah. She sighed, then she began to sing the summer song again. Far off in a field, a meadowlark sang, too.

rustle Small sounds of movement.

Icumen (pronounced a-cum-en) A way to say "coming."

Lhude sing cuccu Loudly sing cuckoo.

seals Large sea animals with paddlelike flippers.

meadowlark A yellow-breasted song bird that lives in low, grassy fields called meadows.

Discuss the story with your class and the teacher. You may want to use the questions below to help you.

1. Why do you think Caleb asks his sister over and over if their mother sang every day? What did she sing about (see page 123)? Why does Caleb want to remember his mother's songs? Why do you think Papa stopped singing after their mother's death (pages 123 and 124)? What reason does he give?

2. How does Anna describe Caleb as a newborn baby? What does she compare him to? Do you see humor in her comparison? Explain. How did she really feel about Caleb at the time? Why? What little thing did he do that finally won her love (page 123)?

3. Tell about the day of the funeral. Did the relatives who came to the house bring them much comfort? Explain.

4. How did Papa show his love for his children after their mother's death?

5. What made Papa tell Caleb and Anna about Sarah? Why did Papa place an advertisement in the newspaper? How do the children react to Sarah's letter? Why do you think Anna wants to know if Sarah can sing?

6. What details about Sarah's life do you find out about her from her letter? What kind of person do you think she is?

7. How did everyone react to Sarah, including the animals?

8. Is Caleb afraid that Sarah might not stay long? How do you know? What clues make him think that she will stay? Make a list.

9. Can Anna imagine herself as Sarah's daughter? How do you know?

10. What do you think it means that they all sang a song at the end of the story? Why was this so important?

11. Look back at the diagram of the different kinds of love that you made (see page 112). Which of these kinds of love are present in the story? Are there any other kinds of love in the story that you did not think of before? What are they? Discuss.

WITH A SMALL GROUP ▼

Complete the following activities with a small group.

1. We know from the story that it has been several years since Mama's death. How do we know that this family still deeply misses her? Give the details from the story that show that each of the following characters misses Mama. With your group, make a chart similar to the one below. Have one member of your group do the writing.

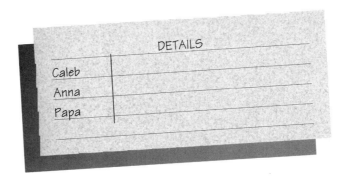

	DETAILS
Caleb	
Anna	
Papa	

2. Who is telling this story? How do you know? How would the story be different if someone else were telling it? Have each member of your group pick a character and briefly tell this story from that character's point of view (see also Unit 2, page 44). You may need to reread the story to decide what your character will say. You may want to have your classmates help you get started by talking about what kinds of things you might say while pretending to be your character.

WITH A PARTNER ▼

Think about the questions below. Discuss one or both of them with a partner.

1. On the day her mother died, what did Anna forget to say to her? How do you think she felt about this? Have you ever felt the same way because you forgot to say something until it was too late? Tell about the situation and how it made you feel. Is there a lesson here?

2. Anna's mother thought that Caleb was beautiful when he was born. Anna thought he was homely and plain. Why do you think their feelings about Caleb were so different?

Try one or both of the activities below.

1. Pretend that you are Papa. Write an answer to Sarah's letter (pages 124 and 125). What will you say? Share it with a partner. Ask your partner to pretend to be Sarah and answer your letter. You and your class may want to display the letters and answers.

2. Begin where the story ended and write a continuation of it. Such a continuation is often called a sequel. In your sequel, write about what happens to the characters. Does Sarah stay? If so, what happens to them as a family? Include some of their conflicts, joys, and any pain they might experience. Share your story with a small group.

You might want to read the whole novel *Sarah, Plain and Tall* to see how close your sequel came to what really happened in the book.

Like the family in the story, most of us have lost someone or something we have loved. This loss may have brought us great sadness or grief. In your journal, write about a time when you experienced grief. It may have been a serious loss such as the death of a loved one or the loss of something you really wanted. Tell about the situation that caused you to be sad and the feelings you had. Describe how you were able to get through the grief and what you may have learned from it. Remember to place the date by your entry and state your topic (see the example on page 16). If you want to, you can share what you write with a partner. Make up your own questions to ask.

USING COMPARISONS ▼

We know from Unit 3 that authors use comparisons to make the meaning of their writing clearer to the reader. In their comparisons, authors often compare two things that are not usually compared. For example, Anna compared her baby brother to a ball of bread dough. Babies are not usually compared to bread dough. With a partner, see if you can find other such comparisons from the story. Write them down and discuss them.

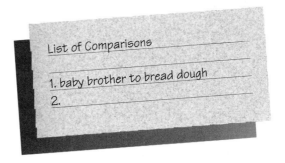

List of Comparisons

1. baby brother to bread dough
2.

Do you think the use of these comparisons helped you to enjoy the story more? Discuss with your class and the teacher.

We know that the feeling of love is difficult to capture in words. It seems to be a bit mysterious. The following poem tells of the mystery of love between a child and a grandfather. As you read, think about how the poet helps you to feel this kind of love.

mysterious Not understood easily.

In the Blood

Pat Mora

The brown-eyed child
and the white-haired grandfather
dance in the silent afternoon.
They snap their fingers
to a rhythm only those
who love can hear.

WITH YOUR CLASS

Discuss the poem with your class and the teacher. You may use the questions below to help you.

1. How do we know that the child and the grandfather feel love for each other? What do they do together? Discuss the meaning of "They snap their fingers together to a rhythm only those who love can hear."

2. Talk about the title of the poem. What does it mean? Does being related by blood strengthen love? If so, in what ways? Is it necessary to be related by blood to have such a strong relationship? Think about what you learned from Unit 3 about family connections.

Try one of the following activities.

1. Find another poem that shows love between family members. It may be love between mother and child, between sister and sister or sister and brother (known as "siblings"), and so forth. Your school librarian, your teacher, or a classmate may be able to help you in your search. Either draw pictures to go along with your poem or cut pictures you like out of old magazines or newspapers. Read the poem aloud to your class or a small group and show them your pictures.

2. Write your own poem about love between family members. Make a drawing to help illustrate it. Instead of a drawing, you may want to cut pictures out of old magazines or newspapers to illustrate your poem. Read the poem aloud to your class or a small group and show them your pictures. You may want to display them in your classroom.

Another face of love is the love we show to all living things. Read the brief story below to see how even a small act of love can be important.

Making a Difference

Sue Patten Thoele

Hawaii The largest island in the Hawaiian Islands in the North Pacific.

ferocious Wild; violently cruel.

ashore Upon the land.

commented Remarked or stated.

knowing smile A smile that shows knowledge, wisdom or understanding.

One day in Hawaii a ferocious storm washed hundreds of starfish ashore. A woman, on her morning walk, bent down every few steps to throw a starfish back into the sea. A man saw her and commented, "There are so many of the poor things it can't make any real difference for you to throw these few back." With a knowing smile, she tossed another starfish into the water and turning to the man said, "It made a difference to that one."

WITH YOUR CLASS

Discuss the following questions with your class and the teacher.

1. What was the man's opinion about throwing the starfish back into the sea? How does it differ from the woman's opinion? Does this tell you anything about how each looks at life?

2. What kind of love is the woman expressing? How is this kind of love different from the love between one person and another? How is it similar?

3. How can this kind of love make a difference in the world? What kind of everyday actions can show this kind of love? Do you think that caring for and protecting our environment can show this kind of love? If so, how?

WITH A PARTNER

List some small things you do with great love. Share your list with a partner.

A LIST OF SMALL THINGS

—write letters to my aunt
—brush my cat
—water my plants
—recycle cans

IDEA BOX

DEVELOPING YOUR WORD BANK

Continue developing your Work Bank. See the directions on page 24.

Choosing a Song of Love

Choose a song about one of the faces of love you have read about in this unit. Write the words to the song and make enough copies for everyone. Your teacher may be able to make copies for you. Bring in a recording of your song and play it for your class. You may want to choose a song sung in another language. If so, make an English translation for your classmates.

Making a Photo-Essay

Make a photo-essay about love. Choose photographs of people, pets, places, or activities that you love. They may be photographs that you have taken or pictures cut out of old newspapers or magazines. Write a description of each picture and tell why it is special for you. Share your photo-essay with a small group.

Writing an Advice Column

Pretend you are an assistant to a famous advice columnist Dr. Anne. Read the following letters and write an answer to each one. Notice that each letter is about a different kind of love. Share your answers with a small group.

Dear Dr. Anne,

I can't seem to get this boy in my science class to talk to me. I try to get his attention by wearing clothes I think he will like and by saying things to attract him. Nothing seems to work. I did catch him staring at me one day, but when I am near him, he ignores me. What can I do? I think I am in love with him.

Love Sick

Dear Dr. Anne,

Everyone seems to have friends except me. They laugh and talk all the time. But me, I am alone. Do you think it might be because I am boring? I just can't seem to think of anything interesting to say when I'm with someone. I try to act cool so no one will know what I am really feeling. I think I'll go crazy if I can't have at least one friend who likes me. Help me please.

Only the Lonely

Dear Dr. Anne,

Two weeks ago my dog died. My parents gave her to me when I was four years old. She was my dog for thirteen years.

I can't seem to stop crying and feeling sad. My parents say it is time to stop thinking about my dog. They tell me to get busy with other things. I don't feel like doing anything. What do you think is wrong with me?

Still missing Muffin

Writing for Readers' Theater

With a small group, rewrite the story "Sarah, Plain and Tall" for readers' theater (see page 75). Change it from a story to a play with characters who talk to each other. You may want to use "Katrin's Present" (page 60) as a guide.

Act it out in a readers' theater. After practicing several times, you and your group may want to present it to your class. Your class may want to videotape it for future viewing.

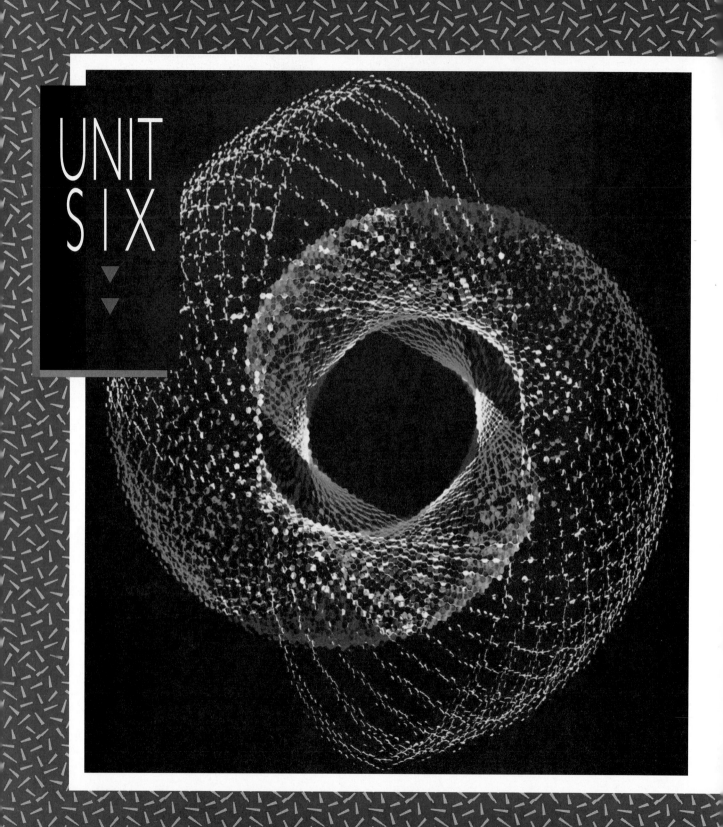

UNIT
SIX
▼
▼

Worlds Together

Every group is a world of its own. Maybe the people in the group all have the same skin color or race. Maybe they all belong to the same religion. Maybe they all live in the same neighborhood. Sometimes groups do not get along with each other very well—one race might fight against another, one religion against another or one neighborhood group against another.

Can different groups learn to live together in peace? That is what this unit is all about.

Choose

Carl Sandburg

The single clenched fist lifted and ready,
Or the open asking hand held out and waiting.
Choose.
For we meet by one or the other.

The main reading in this unit is about a man of peace, Martin Luther King, Jr. What do you already know about this man? With your class, make a learning chart like the one below. In the first column, tell what you and your class already know about him. Then look at the photos and the titles in the different parts of the reading. What do you think you and your class will learn? Write these things in the second column. After you have finished the reading, write what you have learned in the third column.

A LEARNING CHART

What we know already about Martin Luther King, Jr.	What we think we'll learn from the reading	What we learned from the reading

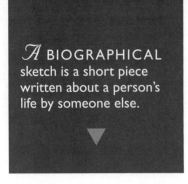

vision Here it means an idea for the future.

justice Fairness under the law.

prejudice Here it means an unfair opinion about something or someone. It is often based on fear and mistrust.

nonviolent Peaceful.

movements Causes that are supported by many people.

swept Past tense of sweep, meaning to move across.

rights Here it means advantages given by law.

equality Being equal or having the same advantages of others.

Martin Luther King, Jr. was a person with a vision. His vision was to bring together two worlds within the United States: the world of African Americans (also called black Americans) and the world of white Americans. In the biographical sketch below, you will see that his goal was justice for all. He hated prejudice of any kind. His nonviolent ways were greatly admired by many people all over the world.

from

Martin Luther King, Jr. and the March Toward Freedom

Rita Hakim

MOVEMENTS are born when many people share a belief that things must change. But every great movement needs a leader. Often, it takes a single person to shape a clear vision of how the world can be.

In the 1960s, a great movement swept the United States. People around the nation realized that society did not treat all of its citizens fairly. They got together to demand equal rights for all.

The basic rights of citizens are called civil rights. In the 1960s, black Americans led the fight for civil rights. Many people had different ideas about how to win these rights. But one man came forward to lead them. His name was Martin Luther King, Jr. His dream was the dream of everyone involved in the civil rights movement: peace, justice, and equality.

THE EARLY YEARS

Martin Luther King, Jr. was born on January 15, 1929, in Atlanta, Georgia. He lived in a house with his mother, father, sister, brother, grandmother, and grandfather. His father, Martin Luther King, Sr. was a Baptist minister. He was a serious, intelligent man who believed in justice for black people. In the South, if a black family wanted to go to a restaurant, they had to sit in a separate section. If they wanted to see a movie, they had to sit way in the back of the balcony. Blacks even had to use separate public water fountains marked "For Colored Only."

Once when his father took Martin to buy some shoes, the clerk made them go to the back of the store. "We don't serve colored in the front of the store," the clerk told them. His father was filled with anger. "If you don't serve colored in the front of the store, then you don't serve these colored at all!" he told the clerk. He took Martin by the hand and left.

Martin learned dignity from both his parents. White people might be cruel to him, but he would not show anger or hatred. His mother told him, "You're as good as anyone." And he believed it.

Martin was the best student in his class. By the time he was 14 years old, he seemed to be taking after his father. He liked his studies, and he liked speaking in public. His father thought Martin might make a good minister.

That year, Martin and his speech teacher, Mrs. Sarah Bradley, traveled across the state to a competition where he gave a speech called "The Negro and the Constitution." The judges were surprised that this 14-year-old boy spoke so well and so seriously and gave him a prize. Mrs. Bradley was overjoyed, and Martin was proud of himself.

They boarded the bus to go back to Atlanta, but soon there

Baptist minister A leader of a Baptist church (a type of Christian church).

South The southern part of the United States.

balcony A flat surface built out from an upstairs wall.

Colored A word meaning black people. It is not often used now.

dignity Showing respect for self and others.

taking after his father Being like his father.

competition Contest to see who is the best.

Negro Word meaning a black person. It is not often used now.

Constitution Here it means the laws of the United States.

overjoyed Very happy.

boarded Got on.

was a problem. Some white people boarded the bus, and the driver told Mrs. Bradley and Martin to move so that the whites could have their seats. There were laws in the South that kept blacks separate from whites. One of these laws said that blacks had to give up bus and train seats to whites.

Martin did not want to give up his seat but Mrs. Bradley forced him to do it. Afterward, he burned with anger and shame. He had just given a speech about the rights that blacks have as citizens of the United States and, now, he was being denied one of those rights.

"That night will never leave my memory," he said later. "It was the angriest I have ever been in my life."

COLLEGE

Martin wanted to do something about the unfair laws, but for now all he could do was continue his studies. He finished high school when he was just 15 years old and went on to Morehouse College in Atlanta, where he continued to be a serious student. There, he decided once and for all that he wanted to be a minister. He made up his mind to attend another school, the Crozer Theological Seminary in Pennsylvania, to continue his religious education.

At Crozer, Martin read many books that influenced his thinking. The most important was a book about Mohandas Gandhi, the great leader from India. (See photo on top of next page.) Gandhi believed in using love, not hate, in the struggle against India's enemies. Martin decided that this was the only way blacks could get justice in the United States.

After Crozer, Martin went on to Boston University. There he met a smart and attractive young woman named Coretta Scott who was studying music. Martin liked her

denied Not given.

college A place where people go to continue their education after high school.

Theological Seminary A religious school where people study to be ministers.

influenced Had power over.

university Similar to a college but usually larger.

British Empire The lands owned and controlled by Great Britain.

resistance Working against something.

determined Having a strong will.

A tiny, smiling man who wore a simple white robe—that was Mohandas Gandhi. He carried no weapons and commanded no army. Yet he forced the great British Empire out of India. Gandhi knew that the British Empire was powerful. Indians could not fight the British with guns. But Gandhi had another plan. He organized Indians and told them not to obey laws that were unfair. He also told them not to fight back. His method was known as nonviolent resistance.

right from the start and asked her out on a date. On their first date, Martin announced that he wanted to marry her. Coretta was shocked, but she soon learned to love this serious, determined man.

THE MINISTER AND THE BOYCOTT

Martin and Coretta were married in the summer of 1953. They moved back to the South the following year when Martin received an offer to be a minister in Montgomery, Alabama, at the Dexter Avenue Baptist Church. He felt that things were changing in Montgomery. Blacks were talking about what they could do to make society more equal.

On December 1, 1955, a black woman named Rosa Parks took the first step. She refused to give up her seat on a bus to a white man and was arrested. Martin and the other black ministers in Montgomery preached to their congregations about having a boycott. They explained the situation and asked people not to ride the buses, but Martin was worried. He knew that most blacks did not have cars and that they depended on the buses to get to work.

On the day of the boycott, however, almost every black in town stopped riding the buses. They walked, or got lifts, or rode on mules or horses. The boycott was working. At last, in November 1956, the Supreme Court decided that Montgomery's bus segregation law was wrong. It went against the U.S. Constitution, which guarantees people certain rights. Montgomery's blacks had won a major victory.

THE MARCH ON WASHINGTON

Now the civil rights movement was at its peak. Millions of people all across the country understood that change must come. On August 28, 1963, a great demonstration was held in the nation's capital: the March on Washington. Nearly 250,000 people poured into the city. They marched through the streets and headed for Lincoln Memorial. The huge crowd gathered around the statue of Abraham Lincoln who

society People who share laws, customs, and so forth; the public.

preached Spoke.

congregations Groups of church members.

boycott An action by a group not to use a service or not to buy something.

lifts Rides.

segregation Separation.

peak The highest point.

demonstration A public show of feeling or opinion.

capital The place where the government is.

poured Here it means came into.

headed Went in the direction of.

statue A figure of a person that is made of clay, stone, metal, or some other solid material.

had freed the slaves one hundred years before. Now the descendants of slaves, America's black citizens, were demanding true equality.

Martin Luther King, Jr. gave his famous "I Have a Dream" speech to the crowd. In it, he captured the hopes and dreams of millions of Americans, black and white.

Cheers rang out when he finished and people hugged one another and wept for joy. Martin Luther King, Jr.'s dream was wonderful to behold.

descendants Children, grandchildren, and so forth.

civil war A war within a country.

captured Took control of.

behold A word meaning to look at. It is not used very much any more.

The "I Have a Dream" Speech

On August 28, 1963, Martin Luther King, Jr. gave one of the great speeches in American history. Nearly 250,000 people had gathered at the Lincoln Memorial in Washington, D.C. They had come together to demand equal rights for all.

Martin Luther King, Jr. spoke to them and to millions of other people watching on TV. He began reading his prepared speech, but then he stopped and put away his notes. He did not need to read. What he wanted to say was in his heart. All his life he had witnessed racism. Now was his chance to present his vision of equality to the nation and the world.

"I have a dream!" he cried. "I have a dream that one day . . . sons of former slaves and sons of former slave owners will be able to sit down together at the table of brotherhood. . . . I have a dream that my four little children will one day live in a nation where they will not be judged by the color of their skin but by the content of their character.". . .

The crowd was struck by his words. He said he dreamed that one day there would be freedom for the whole country. And on that day everyone would join hands and sing . . . , "Free at last! Free at last! Thank God Almighty, we're free at last!"

witnessed Seen and sometimes experienced.

racism A belief that one's own race is best.

content What is in something or what it contains.

character The qualities that someone has.

struck Moved to emotion or strong feelings.

inventor A person who
creates new things.

Later, in 1964, Martin was told that he had won the
Nobel Peace Prize, one of the world's highest honors. He
and Coretta traveled to Norway, where he was awarded the
prize. He was now one of the most loved and respected men
in the world.

Martin Luther King, Jr. received the Nobel Peace Prize in Oslo, Norway.
Coretta is by his side.

THE END IN MEMPHIS

As the 1960s went on, the United States became involved in a war in Vietnam. Martin Luther King, Jr. believed that this was an unjust war, and he said so. Some people told him he should speak only about the problems of blacks, but Martin answered that he had to speak out. "I am a citizen of the world," he said. He was also concerned about all the poor people in the United States, both black and white. In 1968, he traveled to Memphis, Tennessee, to march with sanitation workers who were underpaid. Two nights before the march, when Martin gave a speech, he seemed in a strange mood. He said that freedom was sure to come, but he also said that he was not sure whether he would be alive to see it.

The next day, Martin walked out onto the balcony of the motel where he was staying. A shot rang out, and Martin slumped down. A friend bent over him and tried to help him. But it was too late. Martin Luther King, Jr. was dead.

The convicted killer, James Earl Ray, was a white drifter. He was one of many people filled with anger and confusion in those troubled days. Martin had received many death threats, and there was much hatred in the country. The night before, he had seemed to know that his end was near.

Around the country, people peacefully mourned the fallen leader. But many other people who were confused and frustrated turned to violence. There were riots in many cities and it seemed that Martin's peaceful way might be forgotten.

But it was not forgotten. Since 1986, the United States has officially celebrated Martin Luther King, Jr. Day. Every year on January 15, Martin's birthday, people honor his memory. They remember him as one of the nation's greatest leaders. He was a man who led not with guns, but with words of hope. He was a man who dreamed.

As WE learned earlier, the war in Vietnam was fought between North Vietnam and South Vietnam between 1957 and 1973. The United States went in to help the South in 1965. Many people thought that the United States should not have fought there because it was a civil war within Vietnam.

unjust Not fair.

sanitation workers People who do the cleaning and pick up or collect garbage in cities.

underpaid Not paid enough.

convicted Found guilty of a crime.

drifter Someone who wanders or moves from place to place.

confusion Not knowing what to think or do; being very uncertain.

threats Warnings of harm.

mourned Felt grief.

riots Scenes of violence caused by uncontrolled and angry crowds of people.

officially Formally.

WITH YOUR CLASS ▼

Think about the reading. Discuss it with your class and the teacher. The questions below may help you.

1. Tell about the great movement that swept the United States in the 1960s. Why do you think this movement took place?

2. What did Martin Luther King, Jr. want to do for the movement?

3. Describe Martin's childhood. Did he experience a lot of prejudice? Tell about one or two of his early experiences with prejudice.

4. How did Martin learn dignity from both parents? Why do you think this was so important to him?

5. Which experience made Martin the angriest he had ever been in his life? Why do you think this experience made him so angry?

6. What did Martin learn from the writing of Mohandas Gandhi? Describe Gandhi's method of ending conflict. Why do you think it worked so well for him?

7. Tell about Martin's romance with Coretta Scott. How did she react to this attention? How did the romance end up?

8. Describe the Montgomery bus boycott. Why did it happen? What was the result?

9. What happened during the March on Washington in 1963? What was the climax or high point of the march?

10. What was Martin's dream? Why did he throw away his prepared notes when talking about his dream?

11. What high honor did Martin receive in 1964? Why do you think he received it?

12. Tell about Martin's death. How did he die? Why do you think he died? Did he know beforehand that this was going to happen? How do you know?

13. How did people react to his death at first? How do they remember him today?

With your class, complete the chart you started before the reading. Fill in the third column.

WITH A SMALL GROUP ▼

With a small group, make a chart similar to the one below. Have one member of your group do the writing.

Find details from the reading that show that . . .

	DETAILS
Martin Luther King, Jr. was an excellent student.	
He was a man of peace, not violence.	
He was loved and respected by the people.	

WITH A PARTNER

Think about the questions below. Discuss one or more with a partner.

1. Martin Luther King, Jr.'s mother told him, "You're as good as anyone" (page 146). Why was this a good thing for her to say at this time in his life? Is there anything else she could have said that would have been good for him to hear?

2. Some people did not like it when Martin Luther King, Jr. spoke out against America's involvement in Vietnam. They said that he should only speak about African Americans. He told them "I am a citizen of the world." What does it mean to be a citizen of the world? Do you think his answer was a good one? Why or why not? Are other people citizens of the world? How?

3. Have you or anyone you know ever experienced prejudice similar to what Martin Luther King, Jr. experienced? Tell about the situation. How did it make you or the person you know feel at the time? What about now?

Write your own "I Have a Dream" speech. It may be about one dream or about several dreams. You may want to repeat the words "I have a dream . . ." or "I wish . . ." or similar phrases in your speech. Think about what you would like the world to be like. It could be a world without hunger, a world without war, and so forth.

WITH A SMALL GROUP

Read your speech to a small group. Instead you may want to record your speech on a cassette and play it for your group. Ask your group to make a list of the ideas they feel to be most important in your speech. They may need to hear the speech more than once. Then ask them what they think of your ideas. Do they agree with them? Why or why not? What do they like about your speech? Can they suggest any ways you can improve it? You may want to rewrite your speech based on what you learn.

Looking at Literature

A TIMELINE ▼

Biographies are often written in the order of the events that happened. This order of events is called a *timeline*. The timeline may begin with the person's birth and end with the person's death.

With a partner, make a timeline on your paper of Martin Luther King, Jr.'s life. See the example started for you below.

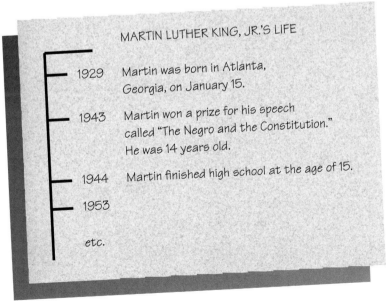

MARTIN LUTHER KING, JR.'S LIFE

1929   Martin was born in Atlanta, Georgia, on January 15.

1943   Martin won a prize for his speech called "The Negro and the Constitution." He was 14 years old.

1944   Martin finished high school at the age of 15.

1953

etc.

We just learned about Martin Luther King, Jr.'s vision for America. In this poem another African American tells about a vision that he has inside his head. Read to see what it is. Do you think all of us can have the same vision inside our heads?

All the Colors of the Race

Arnold Adoff

All the colors of the race
are
    in my face, and just behind my face:
              behind my eyes:
   inside my head.
And inside my head, I give my self a place
  at the end of a long
         line   forming
           it self into a
              circle.
And I am holding out my hands.

race Here it means the whole human race.

WITH A PARTNER ▼

Read the poem again, this time with a partner. Discuss with your partner what you think it means. You and your partner may want to draw what you think the author has within his head. When you are finished, join another pair of classmates. Share your ideas and your drawings.

WITH YOUR CLASS ▼

What if all the people in the world had the author's vision within their heads. Would the world be a different place? If so, how would it be different? Discuss with your class.

STRANGE FORMS OF LANGUAGE ▼

Sometimes writers will use forms of a language that seem strange to some readers. For example, the author of "All the Colors of the Race" separates the word "myself" into two words—"my" and "self"—and the word "itself" into "it" and "self." Did the use of these unusual forms bother you? Why or why not? Why do you think the author used them?

Sometimes we become discouraged because we can't always reach our goals, at least not when we work alone. In the fable below, we learn the power of working together with others.

The Bundle of Sticks

Aesop

disturbed Upset.

arguing Disagreeing or fighting with words.

convince Try to make someone agree with you.

occurred Here it means came into his mind.

persuaded Convinced.

bundle Several things tied together.

straining Trying very hard by overworking the muscles.

snap Break suddenly into two parts.

split Break it in two by causing it to separate down its length.

youngsters Children.

twigs Little branches.

THERE ONCE lived a wise man with three sons. He loved them very much, but was greatly disturbed because they were always arguing. No matter what he said, he could not convince his boys to get along.

One day it occurred to him that the three might be more easily persuaded by action than by words. He called his family together and showed them a bundle of sticks. Can any of you break this bundle in half?" he asked.

The youngest son went first, straining to bend the bundle across his knee. The middle son held one end of the bundle to the ground with his foot and tried to snap the other end with both hands. The oldest son took an end of the bundle in each hand and tried to split it in two in front of him. But try as they might, each of the youngsters failed in turn to break the bundle.

The father untied the bundle and gave one stick to each son. Quite easily, the three sons snapped their individual sticks in two.

"My sons," said the wise father, "each of you alone is as weak as one of these twigs. But if you all stand together, no enemy, however strong, will be able to break you."

Moral: When people work together,
strength is on their side.

WITH A PARTNER ▼

1. Think of two or three questions that will help your partner understand the meaning of the fable. Write them down. Ask your partner to answer the questions in writing and to share the answers with you. Do you and your partner agree on the answers? Discuss.

2. Together with your partner retell the story in your own words. One of you can begin the retelling and the other one can finish. Record the retelling on a cassette. Join another pair of classmates and share your recording.

WITH YOUR CLASS

Return to the moral of the story on page 160. Do you agree with the moral? Why or why not? Could there be another moral? Discuss with your class.

Looking at Literature

THE FABLE ▼

You learned that a fable has a moral. It often also has animal characters in it. For example, in the United States there is a fable told about the tortoise (a turtle) and the hare (a rabbit). Maybe you have heard it. It is about a race that the tortoise wins because he moves slowly but he doesn't stop until he finishes. The hare moves fast but he soon becomes tired and feels he has time to take a nap. What do you think the moral of this story is?

1. Choose another fable that you know of. It may be one from another country. Share it with a small group. Discuss the moral with them.

2. Write your own fable about a lesson you have learned in life. Use the one by Aesop as an example. Decide what the moral of your story is and write it at the end. You may want to draw a picture to help others understand the meaning of your fable. You and your class may want to make a collection of fables.

Look at the picture on this page. What do you think it means?

Can we all work together as one world to solve our problems? The writer of the following song thinks that we can.

from

We Are All One Planet

Molly Scott

We are all one planet, all one people of Earth.
All one planet sharing our living, our dying, our birth.
And we won't stand by watching her die,
Hearing her cry and deny.
We live as she lives. We die as she dies. . . .

So many ways to hurt and not heal,
To speak and not listen, to act and not feel
And too little time to be simple and see
The circle includes every bird, every tree,
every you, every me. . . .

planet Here it means a large body that goes around the sun.

deny To say that something isn't true.

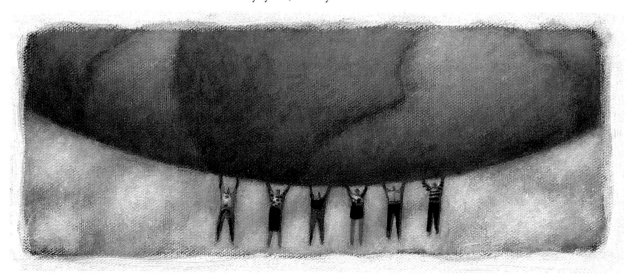

WITH YOUR CLASS

Think about the words to the song. Then discuss the questions below with your class and the teacher.

1. The song writer says that we won't stand by watching the earth die. What does she mean? How might the earth die?

2. What does it mean ". . . to speak and not listen, to act and not feel"? Think of some examples.

3. What are the ways people hurt each other? List some "hurts that do not heal."

4. Why is it important for us to see that our world (the circle) includes "every bird, every tree, every you, every me"?

Before all of our worlds can come together as one, we need to bring people together. What small things can you do in your own family, in your own neighborhood, and in your own school to bring people together? Complete a chart like the one below and share it with a small group.

Ways to Bring People Together

My Family	My Neighborhood	My School
—offer to help my younger brother do a math problem	—invite someone who is different from me to go to a movie	—ask a newcomer in my school to join me on a project in a class we both share

IDEA BOX

DEVELOPING YOUR WORD BANK
Continue developing your Work Bank.
See the directions on page 24.

My Life

____ 19__

____ 19__

____ 19__

Creating Timelines and Biographical Sketches

Earlier in this unit, you made a timeline (an order or sequence of events) for the life of Martin Luther King, Jr. Now make a timeline of your own life. Begin with your birth and include the important events of your life up to the present. To help you organize, first make a list of the important things that have happened to you. Then put them in the order in which they happened.

Now exchange timelines with your partner. Use your partner's timeline to write a short biographical sketch of him or her. Try to find out a few more details about each event on your partner's timeline. Write down some of the details you may want to include. It may be helpful to use some parts of the biographical sketch of Martin Luther King, Jr. as a guide for your own writing. Consider including drawings or pictures of your partner with the sketch. Your class may want to make a collection of biographical sketches to share with others.

Planning a Television Talk Show

With a small group, plan a television talk show about making the world a better place. Have one person be the host and the others be the people interviewed. Choose the people you want interviewed from the this list: Atalanta, San Ho, Pablo Red Deer, Sarah, and Martin Luther King, Jr. Before the talk show, make a list of questions that the host might ask each person.

Exploring a Great Movement in History

The author of the biographical sketch about Martin Luther King, Jr. says "Every great movement needs a leader." Think about a great movement in the country you know best. Was it for more freedom? More rights? A better everyday life? Who led this movement? Find out as much as you can about the movement and its leader or leaders in your school library. Your teacher, the librarian, or a classmate may be able to help you in your search. Share what you learn with a small group. Then write about it. If others in your group are writing about the same movement, you may want to work together as "co-authors." You and your class may wish to put your writings into a collection to share with others.

Forming a Round Table

With a small group, choose a world problem such as hunger, drugs, aids, pollution, war. Find out as much as you can about the problem by using your library for information. Ask your teacher or the librarian, or a classmate, to help you. Come back to your group and share what you have learned. With your group, talk about the problem and what can be done about it. Think about the questions below:

a. What is the problem? Describe it.
b. Who has the problem?
c. What caused the problem?
d. What can be done about the problem?
e. What will happen if nothing is done to help?

Present your findings and conclusions to your class using pictures or other aids to help them understand. Suggest to them ways that they might help solve the problem.

INDEPENDENT READING

Here are suggestions for independent reading about each of the themes in this book.

UNIT 1   A WORLD OF MY OWN

Crazy to Be Alive in Such a Strange World

edited by Nancy Larrick.
M. Evans and Company, 1989.

Poems about many kinds of people and how they feel about themselves and the world around them. It includes the points of view of old people, young people, married people, persons of many different cultures, etc.

The Dream Keeper and Other Poems

by Langston Hughes. Alfred A. Knopf, 1960.

This book of poems is about not being afraid to dream and about making your dreams come true.

Free to Be . . . You and Me

edited by Carole Hart, Letty Cottin Pogrebin, Mary Rodgers, and Marlo Thomas. Free to Be Foundation and Bantam Books, 1974.

Stories, poems, songs, etc. about liking who you are and being true to yourself and your goals. "Atalanta" and "The Sun and Moon" come from this book.

Isamu Noguchi: The Life of a Sculptor

by Tobi Tobias, Crowell, 1974.

A Japanese boy comes to America. As he grows older, he works very hard to become a great artist. He doesn't lose sight of his dream even when life seems to be against him.

The Magic Wings: A Tale From China

by Diane Wolkstein. E.P. Dutton, 1983.

This tale is about a girl who wants to have magic wings so she can fly. The story delights persons of all ages.

Sachie: A Daughter of Hawaii

by Patsy Sumie Saiki. Kisaku, 1977.

Sachie, a Japanese-American girl living in Hawaii, faces many problems and finds herself in conflict with her parents and tradition.

Pathblazers: Eight People Who Made a Difference

by M.K. Fullen. Open Hand Publishing, 1992.

True stories about famous black Americans who knew what they wanted and went out and got it. They often used their talents to improve the lives of others.

UNIT 2   MAKING FRIENDS IN A NEW WORLD

Bridge to Terabithia

by Katherine Paterson. Crowell, 1977.

In this book two newcomers become friends. They live in a pretend magical kingdom where life is wonderful until something very sad happens that changes their whole world.

In the Year of the Boar and Jackie Robinson

by Bette B. Lord. Harper Junior Books, 1984.

Shirley Temple Wong's new life in America is both difficult and humorous. Things don't happen quite as she expects—especially at school.

A Jar of Dreams; The Best Bad Thing; and The Happiest Ending

by Yoshiko Uchida. Atheneum, 1985.

These three books are about a Japanese-American girl in California. She faces the problems of a new world at a time when many people did not even have enough money to put food on the table.

The Me Nobody Knows

edited by Stephen M. Joseph. Henry Morrison, 1969.

This book is a collection of poems written by children from the ghetto. "I Have Felt Lonely" by Arthur Jackson is in this collection.

My Name Is San Ho

by Jayne Pettit. Scholastic, 1992.

Read the complete story about San Ho and his other experiences making friends in a new world.

Free to Be . . . a Family

edited by Marlo Thomas, Christopher Cerf, Letty Cottin Pogrebin, Carol Hall, Sarah Durkee, Wendy Goldwyn, Norman Stiles. Free to Be Foundation/Bantam Books, 1987.

Stories, poems, songs, etc. about different kinds of family groups and the importance of family ties. The song "Free to Be . . . a Family" and the story "Twanna and Me" come from this book.

A Gathering of Days: A New England Girl's Journal 1830–32

by Joan Blos. Macmillan, 1979.

A teenage girl's journal tells how she faced her father's remarriage and her best friend's death.

Annie and the Old One

by Miska Miles. Little Brown, 1971.

A young girl faces the death of her grand-mother. Because of this experience, she beings to understand what life is all about.

I Remember Mama

by John van Druten. Harcourt Brace Jovanovich, 1944

This is the play from which "Katrin's Present" was taken. In it you will see the same family having other experiences that bring them closer together.

UNIT 4 WHAT MAKES A HERO?

Dogsong

by Gary Paulsen. Puffin Books, 1987.

In this exciting adventure story, a young Eskimo leaves his village to find his own "song" and become a man. He travels by dog team across dangerous paths in a land of ice and snow.

How It Feels to Live with a Physical Disability

by Jill Kremetz. Simon and Schuster, 1992.

Here we learn of the lives of many physically handicapped young people and of the courage it takes to survive. The story about Melissa Medrano, which you read in this unit, comes from this book.

Journey to America

by Sonia Levitin. Atheneum, 1970.

This book is the story of Lisa, a young Jewish girl, who leaves her home in Germany just before World War II. In it she shows the courage it takes to leave home and all that is familiar.

Pride of Puerto Rico—The Life of Roberto Clemente

by Paul Robert Walker. Harcourt Brace Jovanovich, 1988.

This biography tells of the baseball superstar from Puerto Rico who was noted for being a hero on and off the baseball field.

Sounder

by William H. Armstrong. HarperCollins, 1972.

A book about the dignity and courage of a boy and his family in the 19th-century American South. This book was made into a popular American movie.

The Tenement Writer: An Immigrant's Story

by Ben Sonder (Alex Haley, General Editor). Steck-Vaughn, 1993.

A Jewish girl leaves her village in Poland and comes to America. But she soon finds that America is not everything she dreamed it would be. This book tells of her problems in her new land and how she was able to overcome them.

UNIT 5 THE FACES OF LOVE

Maria Luisa

by Winifred Madison. Lippincott, 1971.

A beautiful book about a girl's adjustment to a new world. In spite of all her difficulties, she is able to show love to those around her, both at home and in school.

My Brother Sam Is Dead

by James Collier and Christopher Collier. Four Winds, 1974.

This is a book about a family's love as its members have to choose sides in the American Revolutionary War against the British. Family members find themselves on opposite sides in this war.

Lupita Manana

by Patricia Beatty.
Morrow Junior Books, 1981.

Lupita comes to the United States from Mexico without the legal papers she needs. Out of love for her family still in Mexico, she gets a job so she can help them survive.

Sarah, Plain and Tall

by Patricia MacLachlan.
Harper Trophy/HarperCollins, 1985.

Caleb, Anna, and Papa wonder if Sarah is going to stay with the family or return to the east coast which she loves so much. Read the book to find out what decision she makes.

The Sound of Waves

by Yukio Mishima. Alfred A. Knopf, 1956.

This book tells a story of first love. Hatsue is a young Japanese woman, trained to dive for pearls. Shinji is the young man from the fishing village who falls in love with her.

UNIT 6 WORLDS TOGETHER

All the Colors of the Race

by Arnold Adoff. Lothrop, 1982.

The poem by the same name (found in this unit) came from this book. All of the poems in the book are told from the point of view of a child from a mixed marriage: the mother is black and the father is white.

I Am the Darker Brother

by Arnold Adoff. Macmillan, 1968.

Poems about blacks in America and the problems they face in school and on the street.

Fresh Paint: New Poems

by Eve Merriam. Macmillan, 1986.

The poems in this collection are about living with each other in a modern world. Pollution, junk mail, and the importance of action are just a few of the topics included.

When Justice Failed: The Fred Korematsu Story

by Steven A. Chin (Alex Haley, General Editor). Steck-Vaughn, 1993.

Fred Korematsu, a Japanese man, was one of thousands of Japanese Americans put into holding camps in the United States during World War II. At that time Japan and the United States were at war with each other. The story tells of his fight for freedom and for the freedom of other Japanese Americans.

Martin Luther King: The Peaceful Warrior

by Ed Clayton. Prentice Hall, 1968.

This biography of Martin Luther King, Jr., gives a lot of insight into the man, his courage, and his strength.

Rosa Parks and the Montgomery Bus Boycott

by Teresa Celsi. The Millbrook Press, 1991.

This book is a biography of Rosa Parks, who would not give up her seat on a bus to a white person in 1955. Her courage helped blacks win more civil rights in the United States.

Something New Begins: New and Selected Poems

by Lilian Moore. Atheneum, 1982.

A collection of poems mainly about ecology and protecting our planet for the future.

WRITING BOOK REVIEWS

Your teacher may want you to write reviews of several of the books you read. The books you review may or may not be about the themes in this book. For example, you may want to review a book about space missions or about the life of a famous rock star.

The purpose of each review is to tell your classmates your opinions about a book that you have read. In each review, tell what the book was about, what you liked and didn't like about it, and whether you think your classmates should read it. You may write your review on a large index card for a class file or you might put it into a computer data base if your class has one. See the form below.

BOOK REVIEW

Title of book:

Author:

Type of book:

Name of reviewer:

Date:

What did you feel this book was about?

What did you like about this book?

Was there anything you did not like about this book? Explain.

Do you think your classmates should read this book?

Why or why not?

KEEPING A READING JOURNAL

Keep a reading journal. Having a separate journal for reading is a good way to record your feelings about what you are reading. You can tell what you think about the actions of a character. You can give your opinion about something the author is saying. You can tell about your own experiences that may have been like those of the character or the author. Or you might want to talk about *how* you are reading. Is reading easier for you now? What are you doing before you read to help you understand the reading better? Have you discovered a good way to learn new words? Write in your reading journal two or three times a week. Put the date by each entry.

CO-AUTHORING A JOURNAL

Keep a reading journal with a partner. Together choose a book you both want to read. While you are reading, both of you can write in the journal from time to time (see the left column below). You can then respond to what your partner has written (see the right column below). In your responses, you may ask questions, give opinions, etc. Questions can be answered and opinions can be discussed in your next entry. Place the date and your name by all your entries. Your journal may look something like this.

Entries	Responses
Your Name: _____	
Date: _____	
Entry:	
Your partner's name: _____	
Date: _____	
Entry:	

GLOSSARY

A

abound To have a great amount.

absently Without thinking.

absorbing Here it means taking in.

abusing Here it means harming the body.

accident An unexpected event; often an injury.

address Give a speech to.

adjust Change slightly for better balance.

adopted Belonging legally to a family that one was not born into.

advertisement A paid public announcement.

affected Caused something to change.

announcing Making known; spreading the news.

apologize To say you are sorry.

appreciate To value; to be grateful for.

approached Came toward.

arguing Disagreeing or fighting with words.

argument A discussion where there is disagreement.

artillery Large guns.

ashore Upon the land.

attached Connected to.

audience A group gathered to watch a play or other performance.

B

balcony A flat surface built out from an upstairs wall.

banked left Turned to the left.

banners Long pieces of cloth with decorations or words on them.

Baptist minister A leader of a Baptist church (a type of Christian church).

barbecue Meat cooked on an open flame. A sauce is often poured on it for added flavor.

barrio The Spanish word for neighborhood.

Baseball Hall of Fame A place where baseball players are honored.

batted Hit.

bear Cope with or put up with.

behold A word meaning to look at. It is not used very much any more.

blazes Burns rapidly or brightly.

blending A coming together.

blessed Made holy.

blonde Light in color.

boarded Got on.

bold Striking to the eye. Sometimes means courageous.

boycott An action by a group not to use a service or not to buy something.

bread dough A mixture of flour and liquid for making bread.

bride's bonnet A flower in the shape of a bride's hat.

bright Here it means smart; intelligent.

British Empire The lands owned and controlled by Great Britain.

brittle Hard but easy to break.

brooch A pin often worn on a woman's blouse or sweater.

brush Here it means small bushes.

bubbled Formed bubbles on top.

bugle A musical instrument like a trumpet but shorter and more simple.

bulldozers Large machines used to move earth or large objects out of the way.

bunched up Here it means bent together at the knees.

bundle Several things tied together.

burst Sudden movement full of force.

C

calcium A metal that is found in bones and teeth. It is needed for normal strength.

campfire A fire built outdoors to give warmth and cook food.

canyon A long narrow valley with sides that rise sharply.

capital The place where the government is.

captured Took control of.

cargo plane A plane that carries supplies.

casually In a very relaxed way.

challenge A test of courage or skill.

character The qualities that someone has.

characters Persons in a play, novel, or story.

cheap trash Something that has little value; inexpensive junk.

checkers A board game played with colored pieces.

chorus Several lines that are repeated in a song.

civil war A war within a country.

clattered Made loud noises as it hit the hard surface and bounced.

clover Low-growing plants with three leaves.

clump Group.

clung Stuck to; the past tense of cling, which means to hold on to something tightly.

college A place where people go to continue their education after high school.

colt A young horse, not fully grown.

combinations Two or more things joined together.

commented Remarked or stated.

compassion A caring for others who are suffering.

competition Contest to see who is the best.

concentrate To give careful attention.

conch shell A large, spiral shell.

confide Tell private thoughts.

confirmed Supported.

confusion Not knowing what to think or do; being very uncertain.

congregations Groups of church members.

Constitution Here it means the laws of the United States.

contemptuously With scorn or deep dislike.

content What is in something or what it contains.

convicted Found guilty of a crime.

convince Try to make someone agree with you.

cool Nice.

coral Pink rocklike structures formed by a small sea animal.

costume Clothing an actor wears on the stage.

count on him Know that he will do what he promises.

couple a' Couple of, meaning two.

course The path followed by the runners.

coyotes Small, doglike wild animals living mainly in North America.

cracked Here it means made a loud noise like something breaking apart.

crackled Made snapping sounds.

crept The past tense of creep, which means to crawl.

crimson Dark red.

crouched Bent over.

cube of sugar A little square made of sugar.

curiosity A strong desire to learn about something.

darting Making rapid, sudden movements.

dashed Moved quickly.

deaden Soften the sound so it can not be easily heard.

dealing with Taking action about.

debut (pronounced day-byoo) First time.

deeds The things a person does.

delighted Very happy.

demonstration A public show of feeling or opinion.

denied Not given.

deny To say that something isn't true.

descendants Children, grand-children, and so forth.

determined Having a strong will.

dignity Showing respect for self and others.

discouraged Without hope or courage.

disgusted Filled with dislike or disapproval.

displays Shows by holding it up.

disturbed Upset.

dramatic Highly emotional; exciting.

dreadful Terrible.

drifter Someone who wanders or moves from place to place.

dusk The beginning of darkness in the evening.

E

eagerly With a very strong interest.

echoed Was sent back from the walls; repeated.

election Selecting by taking a vote.

embarrassing Making a person feel uncomfortable inside.

emotionally With a lot of feeling.

equality Being equal or having the same advantages of others.

energetic Strong and very active.

every–single–day An expression meaning each day.

exchange glances Look at each other in a meaningful way.

excuse A pretend or made-up reason.

exercise bike A bike that does not go anywhere when a person rides it.

exhausted Very tired.

expensive Costing a lot of money.

F

familiarly Well-known, under-stood.

farewell An old-fashioned word for good-bye.

fate In this case, the final result.

feisty Lively, very active.

ferocious Wild; violently cruel.

flagman A person who uses a flag or sign to slow down or stop traffic where people are working.

fleetest An old-fashioned word meaning fastest.

folks Here it means the people one belongs with.

foothills Small hills at the foot, or base, of a mountain.

foster children Children taken care of by another family until their own parents can care for them again.

fragile Easily broken.

frown An expression caused by displeasure.

fruition Made something good happen.

frustrated Kept from reaching a goal.

gasped Quickly took in a short breath of air.

genetic Passed from the parents to their children through cells called genes. The genes control such things as hair color, etc.

geography The study of the earth.

globes Round maps shaped like the world.

goldenrod Wild plants with yellow flowers.

graduation from the eighth grade In the year 1910, graduations were held after the eighth grade as well as after the twelfth. Many students at that time did not continue school after the eighth grade.

grasped Grabbed firmly.

guava tree A tree having white flowers and fruit that can be eaten.

gunnysack A sack made of a rough brown cloth.

gurgling Sounding like water running unevenly, perhaps over rocks.

handouts Food or gifts given freely.

Hawaii The largest island in the Hawaiian Islands in the North Pacific.

headed Went in the direction of.

hearthstones The stones surrounding a fireplace.

heavily-loaded Carrying a great quantity.

heirloom (pronounced air-loom) Something of value belonging to a family for a long time.

herd A group of animals.

hesitated Waited briefly.

hinted Suggested in a secretive way.

hogan A rounded Navajo house made of earth and wood.

holler A loud cry.

hollow Sounding like a noise made in a place that is empty.

holster A case for a gun which is worn on the body.

homely Ugly; not attractive.

housekeeper Someone hired to take care of the housework.

identity The things that make something different from the others.

images Pictures.

imagination The forming of mental pictures of what is not actually present.

impressed Moved deeply to feelings of respect.

impulse A sudden desire to act in a certain way.

incision A cut made with a knife.

independent Able to live without help from others.

indicated Suggested an action with words or movements of the body.

influenced Had power over.

informal Not formal or following usual actions.

insult A comment intended to hurt someone's feelings.

intend Plan to.

intently With full attention.

inventor A person who creates new things.

J

Jacques Cousteau A French underwater explorer and writer.

Jíbaro (pronounced hee-báh-roh) One who belongs to a special group of Puerto Ricans.

jubilant Very happy.

juniper A green bush.

justice Fairness under the law.

K

kidding Teasing or not serious.

kinda Kind of.

kingdom The land controlled by the king.

knowing smile A smile that shows knowledge, wisdom or understanding.

L

lay hands on To get or acquire.

lifts Rides.

limited Restricted; only having a few.

lugged Pulled or carried with much difficulty.

M

made out Could barely hear.

major leagues The highest level of baseball teams.

making fun of Saying unkind things that cause others to laugh.

Marine A type of soldier who serves both on land and on sea.

marvelous Great.

match An equal.

meadowlark A yellow-breasted song bird that lives in low, grassy fields called meadows.

medals Pieces made out of metal (often shaped like coins) to honor people.

medication Medicine.

meekly Here it means without force or strength.

mild mannered Gentle in the way one acts.

mists Fine rains made up of very small drops of water.

moan A low sound like a soft cry.

motioned Directed by using movements of the body.

motions Actions.

mounted Increased the number of.

mourned Felt grief.

mournful wail A cry full of grief or sorrow.

movements Here it means causes that are supported by many people.

mumbled Said something that couldn't be heard clearly.

murmur A low sound of voices, but the words are run together and cannot be heard.

mysterious Not understood easily.

N

naval base Where people in the navy live and work.

nonviolent Peaceful.

Norwegian-American (pronounced nor-wée-jen) An American who came from Norway or whose relatives came from Norway.

notice Here it means warning that something is going to happen.

O

occurred Here it means came into his mind.

officially Formally.

operation (another word for "surgery") Cutting into the body to repair it.

opinions What one thinks; judgments.

ordinary Common, not different or unusual.

overjoyed Very happy.

P

paddock A small enclosed field, often used for exercising animals.

paintbrush An orange flower shaped like a brush.

pale Light colored.

panic Extreme fear.

pantry A small room off the kitchen where food and dishes are kept.

peak The highest point.

pediatrician A children's doctor.

peered Looked.

persuaded Convinced.

pester Bother or annoy.

phrases A small group of words used together to mean something.

physical therapist A person who has had special training to help people use parts of their body again.

pickup Small truck with a wide open area in the back.

pigeon A common bird.

pitch A tone or sound.

pitcher A container that holds liquids. It has a spout for easy pouring.

planet Here it means a large body that goes around the sun.

plums Round, purple fruit.

pollen Powderlike dust given off by the male part of a plant.

porch A covered entry way built out from the house.

poured Here it means came into.

prairie violet A small purple flower growing on the prairie.

prairie A large area of flat, rolling grassland.

preached Spoke.

prejudice Here it means an unfair opinion about something or someone. It is often based on fear and mistrust.

preparing Getting ready.

prevailed Won or had greater strength.

privacy Time to be alone with no one watching or listening.

proclaimed Said or announced in public.

project A planned activity.

pull ahead Run out in front.

put on Here it means to take on.

 R

racism A belief that one's own race is best.

rascal A worthless person (often used jokingly).

reaction An act in answer to something.

reassuring Calming; causing to feel sure again.

recounted Retold.

reflects Mirrors or gives back an image.

rehabilitation A program to help a person become as active and healthy as before.

related Connected by blood or marriage.

resentful Feeling that someone has harmed you in some way.

residents Here it means doctors who are receiving special training.

resistance Working against something.

resolve Decision.

rights Here it means advantages given by law.

riots Scenes of violence caused by uncontrolled and angry crowds of people.

rippling Moving in little waves.

road crew A group of workers who build and repair roads.

roamer Someone who moves from one place to another a lot.

roots Where he came from; his culture.

rustle Small sounds of movement

rusty Turned orange and rough by the water.

S

sanitation workers People who do the cleaning and pick up or collect garbage in cities.

scallop, sea clam, oyster, razor clam Sea animals having hard outer shells.

scattering Throwing them around.

screeching wail A high, loud cry, often in pain.

seals Large sea animals with paddlelike flippers.

segregation Separation.

set [the traps] Put in a certain position so they will catch and hold an animal that steps on them.

settle down Become quiet and relaxed.

shaken Moved back and forth by a strong force.

shimmered Gave back light.

shock A serious upset to the mind and body caused by a sudden, very unpleasant event.

shot on Moved forward with great speed.

shoved Pushed.

shuffling With a sliding walk.

similarities The ways in which people, places, or things are alike.

siren A loud horn or whistle sound to give warning.

sit-ups Exercises done by lying flat on one's back on the floor and sitting up over and over again.

skeptical Disbelieving.

slab A thick slice.

slumped Fell or drooped.

smug Overly satisfied with oneself.

snap Break suddenly into two parts.

snatching Taking away quickly.

sniff Smell.

sniffing Breathing through the nose while crying.

soar To fly swiftly upward.

soared Flew upward.

sobs Sounds made when crying.

society People who share laws, customs, and so forth; the public.

solo Alone.

sought The past tense of seek which means to look for.

South The southern part of the United States.

split Break it in two by causing it to separate down its length.

squatting Sitting on one's heels.

stagehands People who arrange the scenery and lights in a play.

start me off Have me begin or get me going.

statue A figure of a person that is made of clay, stone, metal, or some other solid.

steadily Evenly, without tripping.

steadying Controlling one's movement.

steep Rising sharply.

step-daughter (stepdaughter) A daughter by marriage.

stepfather The husband of one's mother by a later marriage.

sternness Seriousness, stiffness.

stew A thick soup made of cooked meat and vegetables.

stilled Became quiet.

stirred Moved.

strained Used great effort.

straining Trying very hard by overworking the muscles.

stroked Gently rubbed.

struck Here it means moved to emotion or strong feelings.

struggled Made a great effort.

stubborn Refusing to obey or give in.

stumbled Tripped and almost fell.

suitable Right or appropriate.

surgeon A doctor who operates or does surgery.

survive Stay alive; live longer.

swayed Moved back and forth.

swept Past tense of sweep, meaning to move across.

swiftest Having the greatest speed.

swirling Going around in a circle.

tailgate Here it means the back of a pickup truck that folds down.

taking after his father Being like his father.

talents Activities that people have the ability to do well.

teakettle A covered pot with a spout. Used for boiling water to make tea.

teetered Stood but moved back and forth, almost falling.

telescope A scientific instrument for making objects appear larger and nearer.

tense With muscles tightly stretched.

threatening Promising to do harm.

threats Warnings of harm.

thrusts Pushes with force.

titles Names given to honor people.

toss of her head A movement that involves turning the head back quickly and bringing it forward again.

track Here it means to find him by knowing his smell.

translated Said in another language.

traps Here they are pieces of equipment used to catch and hold animals.

trembled Shook.

troublesome Causing trouble.

trousers Long pants that are usually worn by men.

trumpets Musical instruments made of metal tubes with bell-shaped ends. Music is made by blowing into them.

tugging Pulling.

turnips A round lightly colored root eaten as a vegetable.

twigs Little branches.

twilight The faint light just after sunset.

undaunted Here it means dependable and steady.

underpaid Not paid enough.

university Similar to a college but usually larger.

unjust Not fair.

urged Pushed or strongly encouraged.

V

velvet A soft, furry cloth.

violently With great force.

vision Here it means an idea for the future.

W

wailed Cried loudly.

wife-to-be The wife that he will soon have.

wild asters Wild plants with spear-shaped leaves.

witnessed Seen and sometimes experienced.

woolly ragwort A tall plant with yellow flowers.

worthy Honorable.

wrench away Pull away with force.

wretched Miserable; very unhappy.

Y

youngsters Children.

SKILLS DEVELOPMENT SUMMARY

	1	2	3	4	5	6
Discussing with the whole class	✓	✓	✓	✓	✓	✓
Discussing with a small group (3 or more)	✓	✓	✓	✓	✓	✓
Discussing with a partner	✓	✓	✓	✓	✓	✓
Sharing/comparing work	✓	✓	✓	✓	✓	✓
Making lists	✓	✓	✓	✓	✓	✓
Using charts	✓	✓	✓	✓	✓	✓
Clustering	✓	✓		✓		
Finding details to support an idea					✓	✓
Describing places and/or people	✓	✓	✓		✓	✓
Trying out a specific genre	✓		✓	✓	✓	✓
Creating a chronology						✓
Forming questions	✓	✓	✓			✓
Retelling the story		✓				✓
Providing illustrations		✓	✓			
Sharing a literary work	✓				✓	✓
Role playing/Acting out	✓	✓				
Letter writing	✓	✓		✓	✓	
Writing a new ending	✓					
Writing a sequel					✓	
Speech writing						✓
Writing in a journal	✓		✓	✓	✓	
Writing/performing Readers' Theater			✓		✓	
Autobiographical writing				✓		
Biographical writing						✓
Interviewing	✓	✓				
Choral reading				✓		
Reading independently	✓	✓	✓	✓	✓	✓
Learning about the plot		✓		✓		
Mapping the plot		✓		✓		
Learning about point of view		✓			✓	
Using a different point of view		✓			✓	
Learning about the conflict of a story				✓		
Using comparisons	✓		✓		✓	
Using rhyme or near-rhyme				✓		
Learning about . . .						
the folktale	✓					
lyric poetry	✓					
narrative poetry				✓		
figurative language			✓			
drama			✓			
biography						✓
autobiography				✓		
fables						✓

CREDITS

Text Credits

Page 4, "Truly My Own" by Vanessa Howard from THE VOICE OF THE CHILDREN collected by June Jordan and Terry Bush. Copyright ©1968, 1969, 1970 by The Voice of the Children, Inc. Copyright © 1970 by June Meyer Jordan. Copyright © 1968 by the Village Voice, Inc. Copyright © 1970 by Henry Holt and Company, Inc. Reprinted by permission of Henry Holt and Company, Inc. **Pages 7-13,** "Atalanta" by Betty Miles. Reprinted by permission of Bantam Books, a division of Bantam Doubleday Dell Publishing Group, Inc. **Page 18,** "The Sun and the Moon" by Elaine Loran, from FREE TO BE ... YOU AND ME by Marlo Thomas and Associates. Copyright © 1974 by Free To Be Foundation, Inc. Used by permission of Bantam Books, a division of Bantam Doubleday Dell Publishing Group, Inc. **Pages 20-21,** "True Colors" words and music by Bill Steinberg and Tom Kelly. Reprinted by permission of Sony Music Publishers. **Page 30,** "I Have Felt Lonely" by Arthur Jackson from THE ME NOBODY KNOWS. Copyright © 1969 by Henry Morrison, Inc. **Page 32,** PEANUTS reprinted by permission of UFS, Inc. **Pages 34-40,** from "My Name Is San Ho" by Jayne Pettit. Copyright © 1992 by Jayne Pettit. Reprinted by permission of Scholastic Inc. **Pages 52-53,** "Free to Be...A Family" words by Sarah Durkee, Music by Paul Jacobs, from FREE TO BE...A FAMILY by Marlo Thomas & Friends. Copyright © 1987 by Free To Be Foundation, Inc. Used by permission of Bantam Books, a division of Bantam Doubleday Dell Publishing Group, Inc. **Page 56,** "The Simple Happiness of a Navajo Girl" by Ann Clark from CHILDREN OF THE SUN by Adolf and Beverly Hungry Wolf. Copyright © 1987 by Adolf and Beverly Hungry Wolf. Reprinted by permission of Morrow Junior Books, a division of William Morrow & Company, Inc. **Page 58,** "Twanna and Me" by Orlando Perez from FREE TO BE...A FAMILY by Marlo Thomas & Friends. Copyright © 1987 by Free To Be Foundation, Inc. Used by permission of Bantam Books, a division of Bantam Doubleday Dell Publishing Group, Inc. **Pages 60-72,** "Katrin's Present" from I REMEMBER MAMA, A PLAY IN 2 ACTS, Copyright © 1945 John Van Druter and renewed 1972 by Fulton Brylawski. Reprinted by permission of Harcourt Brace & Company. **Pages 84-86,** "The Man From Puerto Rico: Roberto Clemente" by Mark Daniels. Reprinted by permission of Mark Daniels. **Pages 90-96,** "He-Who-Runs-Far" copyright © 1970 Hazel Fredricksen. Reprinted by permission of Hazel Fredricksen. **Page 100,** CALVIN AND HOBBES. Copyright ©1992 Watterson. Reprinted with permission of Universal Press Syndicate. All rights reserved. **Pages 102-105,** from "My Challenge" by Jill Krementz from HOW IT FEELS TO LIVE WITH A PHYSICAL DISABILITY © 1993. Used with permission. **Page 114-118,** excerpts from LOVE IS A SPECIAL WAY OF FEELING, Copyright © 1960 and renewed 1988 by Joan Walsh Anglund. Reprinted by permission of Harcourt Brace & Company. **Pages 120-129,** from SARAH, PLAIN AND TALL by Patricia MacLachlan. Copyright © 1985 by Particia MacLachlan. Reprinted by permission of HarperCollins Publishers.

Photo Credits

Illustration